The Money Ride

Acknowledgments

I have not attempted to cite in the text all of the sources consulted in writing this book. To do so would require more pages than would be practical. The list would include government departments, periodicals, colleagues and experts in the fields of economics, finance, real estate, investing and psychology.

Many people contributed to this book, and two people in particular contributed to its classroom development: David Jones and Joseph Cavaiola. They have allowed me to work with the students in their Economics classes to develop the Money Ride concepts and test the effectiveness of the teaching approach.

A special thanks to Bill Butler whose patience and help with writing and editing was vital, Dennis Busch for illustrating, Eric Larson for the book design and Doug Burgett for the cover design.

Finally, most important of all…to Diane, Josef and Julia—thanks to your love, support and encouragement, *The Money Ride* keeps on rolling!

Contents

Introduction

Have you ever been to an amusement park? If you have, did you find the Money Ride? If you didn't, you missed the most amazing ride of them all! But don't feel bad if you missed it, because you're not the only one.

The Money Ride is hard to find, by design. It isn't noisy and flashy like the other rides. It's just a giant, plain, box-looking building with an entrance marked "$TART" at one side and an exit marked "FINI$H" at the other side.

It's what's inside the Money Ride that makes it the most fun, exciting, challenging, rewarding and longest ride in the park!

Inside, there's a giant wind tunnel containing a roller coaster with trillions of dollar bills swirling all around you. The fantastic thing about the Money Ride is that from the time you enter until you exit *you get to use and enjoy all the money you grab!*

As you read these pages, you will learn how to use smart money decisions and sound money habits to create the lifestyle you want to live. The valuable, easy-to-remember money tips and tools will help you take advantage of financial opportunities and overcome financial challenges.

So, read on and get ready to enjoy the Money Ride—it's the ride of a lifetime and we are all on it!

The Money Ride

1. The Ride

Welcome!

Welcome to the Money Ride! This book is your passenger guide for making your turn on the ride an unforgettable adventure.

As you wait in line, eager for your turn to begin, you can only imagine what it's going to be like. How wild and radical can the roller coaster ride be? And what about all that money swirling about—all for the taking? You're getting more and more excited as you visualize all the money you're going to grab and all the stuff you're going to be able to buy.

The line shuffles forward and you can hear the shouting, laughter and screams as the people ahead of you disappear behind the big door labeled "$TART."

While you wait, you're frantically thumbing the pages of your passenger guide. The more you read the more you begin to realize that this concept of "use and enjoy all the money you grab" probably won't be as free and easy as it sounds—and you're right.

Like most rides at the amusement park, the Money Ride has rules that you must follow. But unlike the other rides, the rules are not about how old you are, how big you are or even about keeping your arms inside the car.

On the Money Ride the rules influence how much money you will be able to grab and how you can use the money to live a happier life. We will cover these rules shortly, but first we're going to talk about how you can make the most of your turn on the Money Ride.

Making the Most of Your Turn

The Money Ride is called "The Ride of a Lifetime" because your pursuit of financial success is a lifelong adventure.

This passenger guide provides you with information on the fundamentals of money and wealth. Because the basic fundamentals of money and wealth do not change, they serve as a reliable foundation for making smart money decisions and building sound money habits to achieve financial success.

Each passenger on the Money Ride, including you, has his or her own personal definition of what it means to be financially successful. Their definitions are unique, but they all describe a particular quality of lifestyle.

Imagine your lifestyle ten years from now in terms of health, family, home, work, leisure and any other aspects you feel are important to you. Keep your imaginary lifestyle in mind as you read and know that it's not just imaginary, it's doable.

Regardless of how you define financial success, your success will be determined by a lifetime of financial decisions which involve what you know about money and how you behave with money—the know-what and know-how of financial success. There are tips and tools throughout this guide that cover what you need to know and do to make the most of your turn on the Money Ride.

The interplay between knowing and doing helps you set goals, make decisions, and build habits and routines to help you follow through with goals and decisions. Sound money habits are routines you use to deploy your money in ways that help you live a happier, more successful life—like "routine money."

You'll find an example of how to create sound money habits amongst the tips and tools in this guide. Though the example applies to the money behavior of spending, it can be used to create sound money habits related to other money behaviors such as saving, borrowing and investing.

Think About It...

1. The Money Ride is not a real amusement park ride, but is it, in a way, real?
2. Your "Financial Success"—describe your lifestyle in 10 years.
3. How are your financial goals, decisions and habits connected?

2. The Rules

The Grabbing Rules

From the time you enter through the $tart door to the time you exit through the Fini$h door you get to use and enjoy all the money you grab. How much money you grab will depend upon these rules:

1. **If you don't graduate from high school.** You must keep your hands in your pockets and use only your teeth, elbows and knees to grab dollars.

2. **If you graduate from high school.** You are allowed to take your hands out of your pockets to grab more dollars.

3. **If you earn an AA degree or learn a marketable skill/trade.** You are given a small butterfly net to grab more dollars.

4. **If you earn a BA/BS degree.** You are given a medium-size butterfly net to grab still more dollars.

5. **If you earn a MA/MS degree.** You are given a large butterfly net to grab still more dollars.

6. **If you earn a PhD, MD or JD.** You are given a giant butterfly net to grab still more dollars.

7. **If you are a business owner.** You are given a giant butterfly net. You're also allowed to bring your employees on the ride with you and you get a bonus dollar for every dollar your employees grab—your reward for creating jobs.

As you study these Grabbing Rules you can see a connection between your ability to grab dollars and your level of formal education. It's as if you actually get paid to go to school.

"Can't be true," you say? Well it is true and there are data to prove it. Each year, the government keeps track of what everybody in the U.S. earns and spends...how and where they earn it and spend it.

The government data examine different aspects of earning and spending, looking for trends and connections between the two. One of the connections is the relationship between a person's education level and their earnings.

The government survey data compare the median earnings for seven levels of educational advancement, from high school drop out to advanced academic degrees. The data show an increase in earnings with each advance in education level. Based on a decade of data and assuming a 40-year work career, the increase in earnings from one level to the next can be $300,000 or more—*the more you learn, the more you earn.* If you want to learn more about economic statistics, here are two U.S. government agencies that produce the data: the Bureau of Labor Statistics (www.bls.gov), and the Census Department (www.census.gov).

Once you've seen the data supporting the connection between education and income, go back to the question, do you actually get paid to go to school?

We essentially get paid for the time we are in school in a way similar to how professional athletes and CEOs of large corporations receive some of their pay...it's called *"deferred income."*

Deferred income is pay you receive at some point in the future after you have done the work according to some acceptable standard. The government data suggests that you really do get paid at some point in the future for the time and effort you spend educating yourself.

TMR Passenger Tips & Tools #1

Do you know someone who is thinking about dropping out of high school or who actually has dropped out of high school? Well, if you do, go to that person and tell them that you know someone who will pay them $300,000 if they will just hang in there and get their high school diploma.

U.S. Government data show that assuming a 40-year working career, a person with no more than a high school diploma will earn an average of approximately $300,000 more than a high school dropout.

Your Work I.Q.

Your Work I.Q. is all of the education, work skills and personal skills you acquire that enable you to earn an income. There is no guarantee that a diploma or degree alone will translate to more income. The data show the advantage of the education—income connection, but hidden in the data is the equal importance of skill. Earning power is a product of what you know and what you know how to do—education and skill.

You really get paid to acquire knowledge and skills which are marketable—knowledge and skills which employers and customers need or want and will pay for. This means that your Work I.Q. is really your *work product,* consisting of your education, work skills and personal attributes which enable you to be a productive worker.

How much you can sell your work product for depends upon the demand for it and your competition. The better paying the job, the more competition you will face.

Education and work skills, as they relate to a particular job, are easy to define. Personal skills, on the other hand, are more general in their application and are important in all types of work. Personal skills consist of two basic aspects: people skills and work ethic.

Your people skills enable you to interact with your superiors, fellow workers and customers in a positive manner. On the Money

Ride, no matter how smart or well trained you are, it will be difficult to reach your full grabbing potential without people skills.

Your work ethic defines what kind of worker you are—it is your attitude and approach to your work. The stronger your work ethic, the more valuable, reliable and productive a worker you will be.

You will compete for jobs against your fellow passengers, initially based upon your education, work skills and work experience. When these fail to give you a competitive advantage, your personal attributes may mean the difference.

TMR Passenger Tips & Tools #2

What kind of worker are you?

Business owners know that when it comes to hiring workers… "Good people are hard to find."

If you want to be a worker in demand, be the kind of worker you would hire if you were a business owner.

Here are three simple but important things you can do to make yourself a valued employee to a business:

1. Be on time
2. Do what you say you are going to do.
3. Communicate clearly in spoken and written word.

As a passenger, you can optimize your grabbing opportunities if your Work I.Q. has value, purpose and focus. Your work purpose and focus describes how a particular job is important to you and how much time and effort it requires of you. Do you just need the job in order to survive for a few months or is it a path to a life-long career? The actual dollar value of your Work I.Q. is determined by employer demand for your specific *work product*. The purpose and focus of your Work I.Q. enhances your ability to identify and compete for available job and career opportunities. Purpose and focus also fuel a strong work ethic, making you a valued employee.

Like most passengers on the Money Ride, you will likely have many different jobs during your turn. It may take a lot of job sampling before you find the field or job that best suits you. Don't be afraid to try new job experiences—they are an important part of developing your Work I.Q.

Thanks to technology, you will have many job and career opportunities to choose from on the Money Ride. New industries emerge every year, needing educated workers with versatile skills. Be bold, enthusiastic, determined and persistent in your pursuit.

As your Work I.Q. and productivity continue to grow, you will always be in demand. Remember, the more you can learn...the more you can earn.

Your Money I.Q.

No matter how developed your Work I.Q. is, it will only take you so far on the Money Ride.

If you really want to enjoy a successful financial life, you need to realize that your income is only the raw material of financial success.

The key to making the most of your turn on the Money Ride will be your ability to create wealth by dynamically deploying the income that you grab. This will require a type of intelligence which is different from your Work I.Q., and it's called your "Money I.Q."

Your Money I.Q. consists of two parts:

1. Your knowledge and understanding of how money works.
2. Your ability to successfully apply that knowledge to help you make smart money decisions.

Work I.Q. generates income in the form of Grabbing Dollars, whereas Money I.Q. deploys income through smart money decisions to pay for lifestyle and to create wealth. Wealth is property also called "assets," which have a money value, can grow in value or can generate income.

While there is a direct connection between Work I.Q. and income, there is no such connection between Work I.Q. and wealth.

The amount of wealth you acquire during your turn on the Money Ride will therefore be influenced more by your Money I.Q. than by your Work I.Q.

The dynamics of Work I.Q. and Money I.Q. are covered later in this guide. Keep reading, and by the time your turn on the Money Ride begins, you'll have a solid foundation of money knowledge to help you make the most of the opportunities to turn your Grabbing Dollars into wealth.

Think About It...

1. What kind of education will you specifically need to increase your Work I.Q.?

2. Work I.Q=income and Money I.Q=wealth…how can you have both?

3. Write a "Help Wanted" advertisement describing your attributes as the "wanted."

3. Money Dynamics

Money Behavior

Money has three basic uses which are influenced by money dynamics.

1. Medium of exchange—buying and selling
2. Measure of price and value of goods and services
3. Measure of value of an account holding money and/or financial property

Money Dynamics consist of two important aspects of money: Money Behavior and the Rules of Money. Your success on the Money Ride will depend on your ability to align your money behavior with the ride's money rules and use your Money I.Q. to create routines and habits that can help you accomplish objectives and goals.

It is important to be self-aware of how money is important to you. Your money self-awareness should include a healthy respect for money.

Every PAW dollar your earn deserves your attention and respect because it represents a piece of your life measured in units of the time and effort it takes to earn it and the opportunity it can create in your life.

Think about the effort and time it takes to acquire the knowledge, skill and experience to earn a dollar. Use your respect for the time and effort as incentive to sustain sound money behavior to create financial opportunities with your hard-earned PAW dollars.

Once you've have respect for your money, you need consider the Money Person in you that influences your money behavior.

What kind of Money Person are you? On the Money Ride there are two basic types of Money Person: Spender and Saver. Regardless of which one you are, it is important that you are aware of how the

Money Person in you influences your money behavior. The influence can be helpful or harmful to your financial success and the well-being of others who may rely on you for financial support.

It is not about judging yourself or others. You may find yourself behaving like a different type at different times—that's okay as long as you are aware of how your thinking affects your actions. Your awareness of the Money Person in you and your ability to change your thinking will help you develop sound money habits. Sound money habits in turn support positive money behavior designed to help you achieve your definition of financial success.

Once you have developed a respect for your money, considered it's importance in your life and have gotten acquainted with the Money Person in you, you can begin to create sound money habits to support positive money behavior.

A habit consists of three action elements which occur in order: Trigger, Routine and Reward. The trigger stimulates a specific action, the routine consists of specific steps to complete an action or task and the reward is the emotion evoked by successfully completing the action.

Sound money habits are repeating money routines associated with a financial trigger like pursuing a financial goal or objective such as or saving money or paying off debt. The routines consist of action steps you take regularly to enable the efficient use of your money. When a routine becomes a habit it happens almost automatically because of some thought or event that triggers the call to action like receiving a paycheck or saving for a dream vacation.

When a routine is completed successfully, you experience a reward that can be either tangible or emotional or both. Think of the happiness you experience from paying off a credit card or the feeling of pride from seeing your savings account grow. This is how sound money behavior built with sound money habits can enable you to achieve financial goals and realize your definition of financial success. Amongst the Tips & Tools you will find an example of creating the sound money habit of controlling spending.

TMR Passenger Tips & Tools #3

Goals and Objectives

The terms "goals" and "objectives" are often used interchangeably, but there is a clear and simple difference between them. A goal is the destination and objectives are the progressive steps to getting to your destination. For example, if you need $600 six months from now, your goal is having the $600 six months from now. To make progress toward your goal, your objective becomes saving at least $100 every month.

Use the S.M.A.R.T. technique described later in this guide to establish money goals and map your path to achieving goals by establishing a routine of repeatable steps designed to complete a specific objective or task.

The Rules of Money

Money is not as complicated as most people think. You only have to remember three basic rules to guide a lifetime of smart money decisions and choices.

Rule 1: PAW and MAW

On the Money Ride, there are only two ways to make money: PAW (People at Work) and MAW (Money at Work). PAW dollars are the hourly wages or monthly salary you earn at work. PAW dollars are called "earned income."

MAW dollars are used to build wealth in assets like savings and investments. The income generated by your MAW dollars is called "passive income." The earned income from PAW and passive income from MAW is called "cash flow." Cash flow is money which flows into and throughout your personal finances every month.

PAW is your Work I.Q. in action. Action is the key word here because it is not enough to simply grow and nurture your Work I.Q. You must put it into action and sustain your PAW activity with disciplined, consistent work ethic.

Be aware!—don't over-do it. Remember that balancing PAW time with family, friends and fun is vital to living a healthy, happy life. It's a matter of the difference between working to live and living to work.

As you master the dynamic of PAW, you will be able to create opportunities to use your MAW dynamic to grow wealth. MAW is really your Money I.Q. in action.

There will be numerous opportunities to build wealth during your turn on the Money Ride. Each opportunity can feature both promise and pitfalls...without both there would be no adventure! You will grow with every PAW and MAW decision you make, as you learn to recognize and optimize your Money Ride opportunities.

Rule 2: Money Is Limited

This rule is based upon a basic law of economics called the "Law of Scarcity." This law states that as an individual you have a limited money supply with which to try and fulfill a lifetime of needs and wants. You have to decide how each dollar is used and know that once you decide, you exclude all other possible uses for that dollar. This means that every important decision can have a positive or negative ripple effect on everything from your current cash flow to your long-term financial goals. Regardless of whether the impact is large or small, the ripple effect is present in most financial decisions.

This law is universal and everyone—from the poor to the wealthy—must play by its rules. Regardless of how much or how little money you have, your ultimate goal is to efficiently manage your personal finances so that your limited money supply is always "more than enough" money for lifetime needs and wants.

Rule 3: Money & Time

There is a fundamental and powerful connection between money and time, which causes your Money Ride dollars to grow or decay in number and value over time. This growing and decaying is connected to another basic economic principle: The Time Value of Money.

There is a formula for calculating the Time Value of Money. Keep in mind that math formulas are most useful for accurately measuring past changes in the value of money over time. They can also be used to project or estimate future changes in the value of money over time, but no formula can accurately predict the future value of your money—a projection is not a prediction.

The connection between time and money creates two basic kinds of time-connected money and on the Money Ride we call these "Today Dollars" and "Tomorrow Dollars."

Today Dollars are dollars that are available for immediate needs or wants. Today Dollars are a product of income. Today Dollars can

TMR Passenger Tips & Tools #4

Time Value of Money Formula:

$$FV = P(1+i)^n$$

This formula can be used to measure the growth and the decay of money over time. Let's first look at how it is used to measure the decay of money. You'll learn how to use it to measure growth later in this guide.

FV = Future value
P = Present value/principal
i = Interest rate
n = Number of time periods

Using this formula, if you had $100 today (P) and you estimate that inflation will average –3% (i) over the next 20 years (n), what will be the future purchasing value (FV) in 20 years of your $100?

You can calculate the estimate that your $100 will have the purchasing power of $54.38 in today dollars...inflation decay of over 45% in 20 years!

$$FV = 100(-3+1)^{20}$$
$$FV = 54.38$$

come from PAW earnings, MAW savings and investments or from borrowing/debt. Whenever possible, you should avoid using debt as an easy way to generate Today Dollars for immediate needs and wants.

Tomorrow Dollars are dollars which need to be available for future needs and wants. Tomorrow Dollars are a product of wealth created by MAW dollars placed in savings and investments.

Each has its own particular purpose and importance in your Money Ride choices and decisions. This means that when you spend Today Dollars, it will be important to always be aware of the need to accumulate and maintain a supply of Tomorrow Dollars.

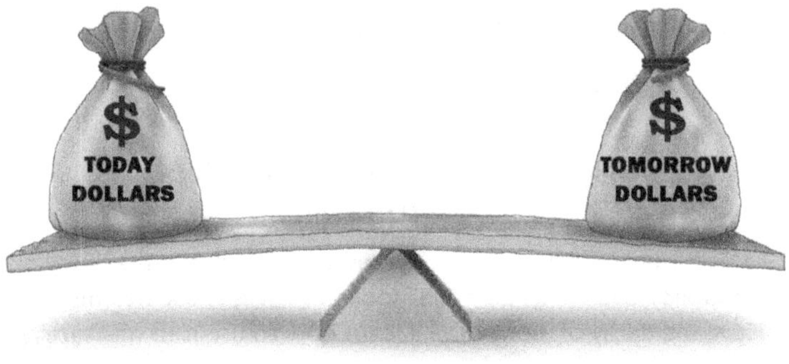

PAW and MAW

On the Money Ride the time–money relationship is always at work, operating through two basic money dynamics: the "PAW Dynamic" and the "MAW Dynamic."

The PAW dynamic is about harvesting—grabbing Money Ride dollars. PAW's impact on your financial success will quickly become obvious to you in your grabbing efforts as you apply your Work I.Q. to gather as many dollars as you can.

The MAW dynamic is about storing and utilizing your harvest of PAW dollars. You will learn to make smart money decisions with your crop of fresh PAW dollars to create a continuous supply of MAW dollars for wealth building.

Efficiency is just as important in utilizing your MAW dollars as it is in harvesting PAW dollars. This is where your Money I.Q.

will take over the stewardship of your wealth building efforts. Your financial success will ultimately be determined by how you apply your MAW dollars to create wealth.

The PAW and MAW dynamics both have the potential to cause your lifetime money supply to grow. Both are also vulnerable to economic forces and events whose impact can cause your lifetime money supply to decay.

This positive and negative potential is influenced by the Law of Scarcity, the Time Value of Money and the fact that the value of money fluctuates like a commodity such as corn or gold.

Money Growth

Growth is the product of opportunities to increase earned income and accumulate wealth. Growth opportunities are created by using your Work I.Q. to earn as much money as possible and then by applying your Money I.Q. in your spending, saving and investing behavior. You will learn more about growing your lifetime money supply later in this guide.

Before considering PAW and MAW growth opportunities and potential, it is important to understand money decay. Important because the factors that cause money decay are always present.

Money Decay

Money is not a commodity like pigs and corn because paper currency itself has no purchasing value. It is called "flat money" because its purchasing value comes from the fact that every dollar is backed by the financial strength of the government—like an IOU from Uncle Sam.

Though currency is not a commodity, it behaves like a commodity because its value can be affected negatively by a variety of decaying economic factors. The factors can affect your money in two ways. They affect your current finances now (Today Dollars) and your future finances later (Tomorrow Dollars). When you lose a Today Dollar, you simultaneously lose the Tomorrow Dollars that the lost Today Dollar could have produced through saving and investing.

Consider the example of the commodity, corn. What happens if corn crop is left in the field exposed to the forces of nature? It will of course, wither and decay or be consumed by pests. However, if the corn is properly harvested, carefully stored and efficiently processed, it can be used to produce a variety of products from food to fuel.

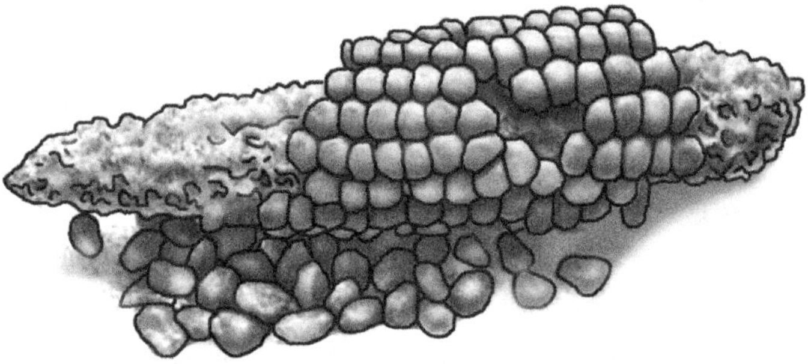

So, what are the factors that, over time, will cause the amount and value of your PAW and MAW dollars to decay, and how do they work?

There are five factors that can cause money to decay: inflation, taxes, interest rates, financial markets, and spending. Inflation affects the purchasing value of a dollar, while the other four factors affect the combined dollar value of all of your money—cash, bank accounts, property, investments and debt.

Inflation is essentially the dilution of the economy's money supply caused by the government increasing the number of dollars in circulation. When the number of dollars in circulation increases, the purchasing value of each dollar decreases—a dollar won't buy as much as it used to. This is due to the fact that there are more dollars available to spend relative to the number of goods available to buy.

Taxes are essentially the transaction fees you are obligated to pay as a citizen. There are five different types of taxes that your PAW and MAW dollars could be exposed to on the Money Ride: income taxes, property taxes, sales taxes, capital gains taxes, and gift and estate taxes.

TMR Passenger Tips & Tools #5

Be Smart About Your Taxes

It's important to know when you might be obligated to pay taxes, but you don't have to become an expert to be "tax smart."

In the early stage of your turn on the Money Ride, your financial situation will likely be simple enough that you can prepare your own income tax return. There are many free or inexpensive internet resources for this level of "do it yourself" tax planning.

But as your earnings increase and you begin to acquire assets, your tax situation will become more complicated. This is when being "smart" often means getting help from a tax expert. The fee you pay for an expert's advice will be worth the money you save by avoiding unnecessary taxes.

You'll pay income taxes as a percentage of the income you earn. You'll pay a sales tax as a percentage of the price of certain goods and services you buy. You'll pay a property tax on the value of real estate you own. You'll pay a capital gains tax as a percentage of the gain you earn when you sell an investment for a profit. Finally, you may have to pay a gift & estate tax on assets that you transfer to your family during your lifetime and at your death.

It is always important to evaluate the tax impact of every important financial decision. Sometimes you can't avoid paying some tax, but by planning the way you earn, spend and invest you can at least avoid paying more tax than is legally required.

Interest rates determine the cost of borrowing money and the interest paid on certain types of investments. The Federal Reserve Bank, a government agency, controls the short-term interest rate used by banks and industry to determine how much you must pay to borrow money. When interest rates go up, the cost of borrowing increases, meaning more of your Today Dollars are spent on loan interest instead of being available to create Tomorrow Dollars by saving and investing.

TMR Passenger Tips & Tools #6

Sound Money Habits

A habit consists of three parts, the Trigger, Routine and Reward. The trigger stimulates action, the routine consists of specific action steps and the reward is the emotion evoked by completing the routine.

For example, with the bad money habit of Senseless Spending ($-S^2$), the trigger is any situation that tempts you to buy something you don't need or can't afford. The routine is your step-by-step reaction to the temptation to spend. The reward is the fun of buying something, even though the purchase represents Senseless Spending ($-S^2$).

Here is an example of how you can create a new habit of Smart Spending ($+S^2$) to replace the destructive habit of Senseless Spending ($-S^2$):

1. Identify the situations or circumstances that act as your spending trigger.
2. Imagine your reward—the positive feeling about yourself resulting from the new habit.
3. Build a new routine of positive action steps to replace the old negative routine.
4. Practice, practice, practice your new routine when your triggers occur!

Start small, working on one habit routine at time. Be patient, it will take time for your new routines to become habit, but your happiness, financial self-reliance and success will be worth the effort.

The decay caused by spending involves two basic types of expenses: lifestyle and financial emergencies. Lifestyle spending covers housing, food, clothes, transportation and everything else you need to live. Emergencies are what they sound like—unexpected events that cost an unpredictable amount.

All lifestyle spending naturally reduces your money supply, but the most destructive form of lifestyle spending is Senseless Spending (-S^2). Senseless Spending includes buying something you can't afford, paying too much or buying solely on impulse. We are all vulnerable to the temptation of Senseless Spending (–S^2). Just remember that if it happens to you it doesn't mean you're a senseless person. It just means that in a weak spending moment you put wants before needs to a degree that can deplete cash flow, undermine your financial goals and jeopardize your financial well-being.

Financial emergencies will happen and you must allow for them in your planning by setting aside money in savings. If you don't, emergency expenses could seriously derail your pursuit of financial success on the Money Ride.

It's almost time! The roar of the roller coaster is deafening now, and as you catch a glimpse inside, you see that there is money swirling everywhere. How are you going to manage all the money you'll be grabbing?

Think About It...

1. How, fundamentally, are PAW & MAW the only two ways to make money?
2. Can you sense how the Money Person in you influences your money behavior?
3. Describe the specific time, effort and opportunity your paycheck represents.

4. Stashing Your Cash

The Opportunity Vest

Regardless of whether you will be using just your hands or the biggest of nets to do your grabbing, you will need somewhere to store all the Money Ride dollars that you will be collecting. You are going to need something a lot bigger than your pockets, wallet or purse to do the job.

No problem—every passenger on the Money Ride gets their very own custom-fitted Opportunity Vest which features specially-designed pockets for storing and deploying your PAW and MAW dollars.

Your Opportunity Vest is where your Work I.Q. and Money I.Q. combine to create the money flowing in, through and out of your personal economy. Money flowing into your vest from income (PAW) and out of your vest to expenses is your *cash flow—cash inflow and cash outflow*. Money that stays in your vest as cash or savings is your *money supply*. Money that stays in your vest as MAW dollars placed in investments is called *capital.*

The vest has three pockets on the front and two large pockets which cover the entire back of the vest. The three front pockets are labeled "SPEND," "SAVE" and "INVEST." The back pockets are labeled "PROTECT" and "BORROW." The vest pockets represent the five domains of your personal finances and money behavior. Every financial decision you make in your life will occur in the pockets on your vest. The vest pockets are elastic and will expand and shrink with your money supply based upon the money decisions you make with each dollar.

In addition to being expandable, each of your vest pockets serves a particular use of money. However, regardless of their specific use, all of the pockets operate according to the rules and dynamics of money explained earlier in this guide.

Because the pockets all operate according to the same money fundamentals, there is a dynamic connection between them. Based upon the law of scarcity, what you do with a dollar in one pocket has the potential to affect the dollars in your other pockets.

Vest Dynamics

Your Opportunity Vest helps you with three important jobs: organizing your financial life, maintaining a stable money supply by managing cash flow, and building wealth through investments.

The vest pockets make it possible to organize your money supply according to the intended use for each dollar. This organization will help you avoid two common and related financial behavior pitfalls which can jeopardize your financial success.

The first behavior pitfall is mentally spending money you have not yet received. The second pitfall is mistakenly planning more than one use for the same dollar.

Allocating portions of your money supply in a particular pocket according to a specific use will enable you to better utilize each dollar. This efficient use of your money is especially important because your lifetime money supply is limited as described by the scarcity of money principle.

The number of dollars in each of the pockets will always be the combined product of your money behavior and the dynamics which grow and decay the value of your money. The combination will create money activity throughout your vest pockets.

The money activity throughout your Opportunity Vest happens in two stages. The first stage is using your Work I.Q. to grab and stash as many PAW dollars as possible. The second stage is using your Money I.Q. to efficiently deploy dollars in the various pockets with smart money decisions and sound money habits to manage cash flow and build wealth.

As long as you are efficient with your grabbing and stashing, you will always have pockets of money to deal with whatever opportunities and challenges come your way on the Money Ride.

The remaining sections of this guide will cover in detail the purpose and dynamics of each vest pocket.

TMR Passenger Tips & Tools #7

The Gravity of Money

Money has a way of behaving like the planets. It's as though every dollar in your vest has a gravitational pull on dollars outside your vest. The more dollars accumulated in a vest, the more pull. On the Money Ride you can witness the gravity of money as money leaves the vest of people who don't manage their money and gravitates to the vest of people who do.

Think About It...

1. Everything you do with your money will occur in your Opportunity Vest pockets.
2. How do decisions you make in your SPEND pocket affect other vest pockets?
3. How might you use your Opportunity Vest to organize your personal finances?

5. The Spend Pocket

PAW at Work

The SPEND pocket is the first stop for every PAW dollar of income you earn on the Money Ride. Decisions you make with your PAW dollars in this pocket are vital to your financial well-being and success—today and tomorrow.

The primary function of the SPEND pocket on your vest is managing cash flow to generate MAW dollars. Cash inflow from your income and cash outflow to your expenses are processed through the SPEND pocket. The process starts with a simple yet powerful question you answer with your actions every time a dollar passes through your hands—*to spend or not to spend*, that is the question!

Think before you answer, and remember that the primary objective every month is to *spend less than your earn*. Your chance for financial success starts with you making spending decisions with a purpose or plan rather than like an unconscious reflex. There are Money Ride passengers who don't realize the difference between conscious and unconscious spending and it makes them vulnerable to the temptation of Senseless Spending ($-S^2$). They lose control of their money, spinning their wheels and end up going nowhere financially—control your money or it will control you!

Every PAW dollar you don't spend can be converted to a MAW dollar for saving and investing. This conversion potential is the real power of PAW and it is unlocked with Smart Spending ($+S^2$). Using $+S^2$ to process your PAW cash flow to create MAW dollars is how you make the important transition with your money from PAW dollars to MAW dollars. On the Money Ride this is called "bridging the gap between PAW and MAW."

Imagine two cliffs labeled "PAW" and "MAW" separated by a bottomless chasm. It is called the "Chasm of Financial Despair" and it's filled with financial mistakes, bad habits and missed opportunities. Your challenge is to build and maintain a bridge across the chasm—a "Wealth Bridge" to get you from PAW to MAW. It's an exciting and harrowing task, but you won't have to go it alone because you'll have help.

Your Friend Bud

Meet Bud, the friendly Money Ride attendant. When it comes to building your wealth bridge from PAW to MAW—do not fear because Bud is here! BUD will help you GET from PAW to MAW—BUD-GET! That's right, your wealth bridge from PAW to MAW is called a "budget."

Maintaining a monthly budget is vital to being financially self-reliant. Your budget will enable you to manage cash flow based on cash inflow from income and cash outflow to pay expenses. Income can come from a job, investments or gifts. Job income is based on what you earn each pay period and is called "Gross Pay." Gross pay minus taxes and other paycheck deductions is called "Net Pay" or "Take-Home Pay." For most working people, net pay is the primary income amount upon which the monthly budget is built.

Your budget cash flow is used to pay for lifestyle expenses and life goals. Lifestyle expenses include everything you need and want to live your lifestyle, such as food, housing, entertainment, clothes, car, etc. Life goals include short-term and long-term financial goals, such as emergency reserves, buying a new car or home and planning for retirement.

Managing your cash flow to balance lifestyle and life goals by spending less than your earn produces excess PAW dollars which you can spend, save or invest. If you save or invest the excess PAW dollars, they convert to MAW dollars which can be used in your SAVE and INVEST pockets.

If you spend the excess PAW dollars, they leave your Opportunity Vest and gravitate to the vests of others. A monthly budget will help you prevent your money from needlessly leaving your vest by keeping track of your spending behavior.

Budget = D^2

There are a number of different ways to design a budget. The most important thing to remember about your budget is that your behavior is more critical than the design. There is a very simple Money Ride formula to help you remember this important point:

$$\text{Budget} = \text{Discretion} \times \text{Discipline}$$

Discretion is the thought you put into making your "to spend or not to spend" choices and decisions. Discipline is sticking to the monthly budgeting process based on your goals and objectives. Discretion and discipline are the foundation of your budget because these two D's enable you to control your money.

Building Your Budget

The basic function of a monthly budget is tracking your cash inflow from income and your cash outflow to expenses, savings and investments. A budget consists of a list of your income and expenses derived from all of your earning and spending data. You will need a system to keep track of all your money activity so that your budget is accurate. A budget system does not have to be complicated, but it should include a procedure and tools for collecting, recording, evaluating and storing all of your transaction data. Each of the tools corresponds to a step in your budgeting procedure, making it easier to establish a budget routine as a sound money habit.

The first tool you will need to create is a data-collecting tool used to save the "source document" from each of your monthly transactions. Your source documents include paycheck stubs, cash receipts, credit receipts and bank slips. This means that every time you earn, spend, borrow, deposit or withdraw money, you save the piece of paper generated by the transaction.

You will need a device where you can stash your source documents from each day when you get home. One idea is to use a piece of wood with a protruding nail, but you can also use an envelope,or

Spending a Dollar

U.S. Bureau of Labor Statistics, Average Annual Consumer Spending, Married Couple + Children

TMR Passenger Tips & Tools #8

Are You S.M.A.R.T. About Your Goals?

1. Write a description of what it is you want as though you already have it. Be **Specific** about what it is and how it feels to know you have accomplished it.
2. List the steps you will need to take to achieve your goal. The steps must be **Measurable** so that you can track your progress...how much...how many, etc.
3. Develop a "can do" attitude about achieving your goal...know that you are deserving of what it is you want and be confident that your goal is **Attainable**.
4. Be **Realistic** about your goal. Be clear that it is something that you are both determined and able to accomplish. Aim high and be real.
5. Give yourself a deadline for achieving your goal so that it is **Timely** in terms of your current situation.

large paper clip. It is, however, best to able to separate your documents into three transaction types: "cash," "credit" and "bank." You can use a single holder or create one holder for each transaction type. Your document holder should be visible and accessible as a habit-building reminder—like your very own Jiminy Cricket budgeting device.

In addition to your collecting tool you will need a tool for recording and evaluating your data. Your tool for this part of your system is called a "budget worksheet." Your worksheet is simply a list of all of your income and expenses. Expenses should be divided into

four main categories: Needs-fixed, Needs-variable, Wants-fixed, and Wants-variable. Needs are things that you must have to live, like food, housing and clothing. Wants are everything else, including amounts to be set aside in savings and investments for future goals. Fixed expenses cost the same amount every month, like rent or loan payments. Variable expenses cost an amount based on how much you use, like food, utilities and entertainment. You can simply list the various categories or divide them into four sections.

In addition to organizing and recording data, a budget worksheet is used to evaluate spending behavior, goal progress and overall financial health. Additionally, categorizing expenses into needs, wants, fixed and variable helps you be more objective about evaluating adjustments to your spending. For an example, see the budget worksheet illustration on page 56.

One expense item deserves special mention: expense reserves. Expense reserves are used to pay expenses that instead of monthly, are paid periodically: quarterly (every 90 days), semi-annually (every 180 days); or annually. The total future amount to be paid is converted to a monthly expense amount. The monthly amount is treated as a fixed expense and transferred to savings each month. By setting aside an appropriate amount in the months prior to the payment due date, the periodic amount due is available in savings when it is needed. Remember to use the expense reserve approach for paying periodic expenses.

Once you have your document holder and worksheet completed you need to create a tool for storing your monthly budget documents and worksheet. For this you can use either a large envelope or a file folder. Whichever you use, on the outside cover label across the top headings: "Month,""Income," Expenses" and "Net +/–". You also will need an envelope labeled with month and year for saving all of your receipts, bank slips, etc.

Your Budget System in Action

The steps that follow describe a manual budget system. Computer software, smart phone applications and websites are convenient and useful for organizing and analyzing financial data. However, tracking your money activity by hand will help you develop the discipline needed to make budgeting a habit. Doing it by hand trains your brain and training your brain is vital to building sound money habits.

Remember the formula, Budget=D^2 The success of your BUDGET will EQUAL your ability to exercise DISCRETION in your spending choices and your ability to develop the DISCIPLINE to stick with the system. Try to follow the system as it is described for at least three months. This will be enough time for you to experience the positive difference a budget can make.

After three months, you can tweak the design and steps to suit you, or switch to a different approach. Regardless of which system you use, the most important thing is that budgeting becomes a lifetime sound money habit.

Here are the budgeting steps:

1. Place your document collector in a high traffic area such as the kitchen counter, bedroom dresser, etc., where you will see it every day as you come and go.

2. Save every source document from *every transaction* you do, no matter how small the transaction amount. Keep every credit and cash receipt, ATM and bank deposit slips and paycheck stubs—every piece of paper for every dollar earned, saved, spent or invested. Place your source documents on/in your document collection tool by transaction category:
   a. CASH nail: Receipts from transactions where you paid with cash, check, debit card, prepaid credit card, gift card or any other cash equivalent.
   b. CREDIT nail: Receipts from transactions where you paid with a credit card, or any form of loan/debt.

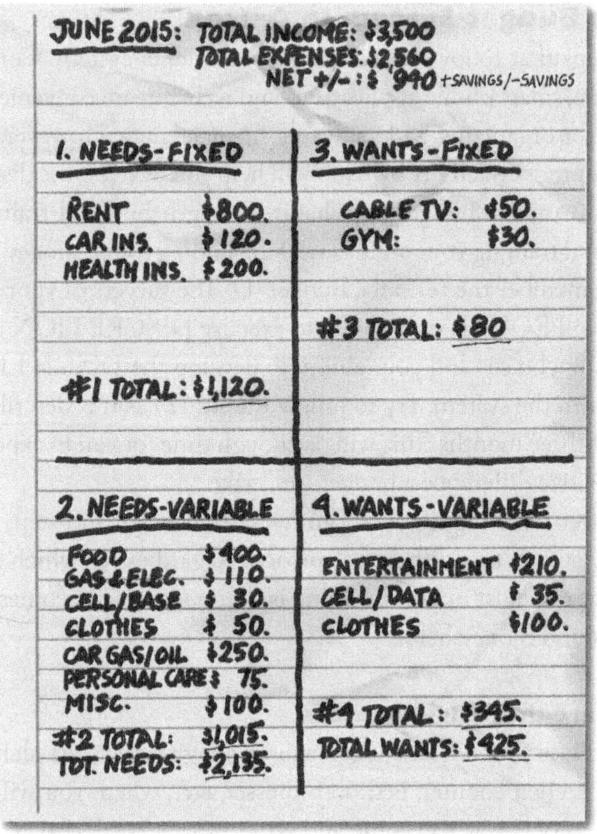
JUNE 2015: TOTAL INCOME: $3,500
TOTAL EXPENSES: $2,560
NET +/- : $ 940 +SAVINGS/-SAVINGS

1. NEEDS-FIXED
RENT $800.
CAR INS. $120.
HEALTH INS. $200.
#1 TOTAL: $1,120.

3. WANTS-FIXED
CABLE TV: $50.
GYM: $30.
#3 TOTAL: $80

2. NEEDS-VARIABLE
FOOD $400.
GAS & ELEC. $110.
CELL/BASE $30.
CLOTHES $50.
CAR GAS/OIL $250.
PERSONAL CARE $75.
MISC. $100.
#2 TOTAL: $1,015.
TOT. NEEDS: $2,135.

4. WANTS-VARIABLE
ENTERTAINMENT $210.
CELL/DATA $35.
CLOTHES $100.
#4 TOTAL: $345.
TOTAL WANTS: $425.

c. BANK nail: Deposit and withdrawal receipts and ATM slips, but not checks.

For any transaction where you do not receive a source document, create one using a small piece of paper listing the amount and category (cash/credit/bank) . Additionally, if it is not obvious from the source, it will be helpful if you note on each document the specific type for a transaction such as "food", "car" or "gift".

3. At the end of the month, using your monthly budget sheet:
   a. Enter your total net pay and other income received for the month at the top of the form at TOTAL INCOME.

b. Take the receipts from your Budget Board and write the type and amount for each source document in the appropriate quadrant on your budget sheet.
c. Calculate the total for items in each quadrant and enter total at the bottom of the section. Calculate the total for the two NEEDS quadrants and enter at the bottom left of the form. Calculate the total for the two WANTS quadrants and enter at the bottom right of the sheet.
d. Calculate the total for NEEDS plus WANTS from the bottom of the form and enter the total on the second line at the top of the form at TOTAL EXPENSES"
e. Subtract TOTAL EXPENSES from TOTAL INCOME and enter result on the third line titled "NET +/–" at the top of the sheet .

4. Using your Budget Folder:
   a. Enter the amounts for TOTAL INCOME, TOTAL EXPENSES and NET in the appropriate columns on the outside of the folder.
   b. Put all of your source documents in the monthly receipts envelope and place the envelope and your monthly budget form in the folder and file it.

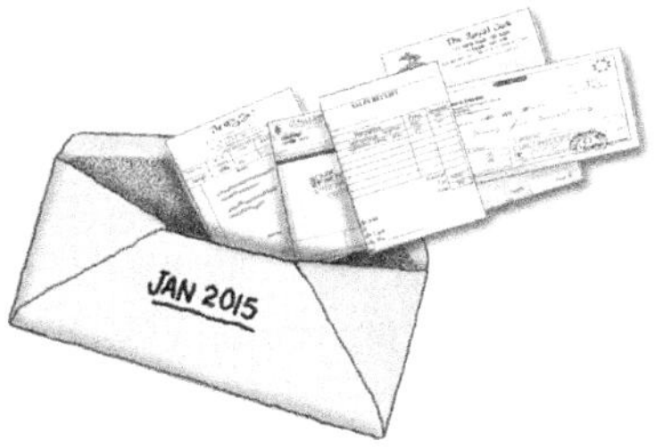

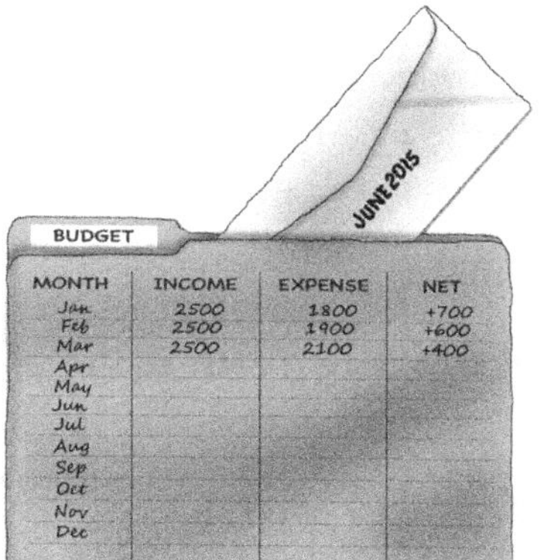

You now know how to design your budget and the actions steps to maintaining your budget. But how do you actually use a budget to achieve your financial objectives and goals?

For example, assume you set a goal to have $1200 in savings in 12 months. Your objective is to save $100 each month. At the end of the first month you managed to save $75 or 75% of your monthly objective. This means that you missed your saving objective by 25%. This could be due to your money behavior or to some unexpected increase in monthly expenses occurred causing the 25% shortfall.

In any month where you either fall short or exceed your objective you can review your budget to adjust your spending behavior as needed. You could review your monthly spending in each quadrant of your budget form to discover the problem expense(s) and make the required adjustment next month to get back on track with your objective.

There is a logical sequence you can use to review your budget. First start with variable expenses in "Needs" and "Wants" where you can reduce your consumption to create surplus PAW dollars. Next, look at "Wants" exclusively and without eliminating all wants, ask your self, "Is there anything in my "Wants" budget that I can live without either temporarily or permanently?" This sequence of analysis will reveal where you need to make adjustments to your spending behavior.

This same approach will also work when you are trying to figure out if you can afford to buy something you need or want. This will work with a need such as a student loan or a car loan or for any "Want". Remember that in all situations, "I can't afford it" can ultimately be a powerful mantra for keeping your spending behavior aligned with your objectives and goals.

Managing Your Bank Account

Managing your bank accounts is not, plays an important role in the budgeting process. In order for a budget to work, you must always know how much cash is actually available in your bank account and it's called your "bank balance".

There are two separate views of your bank balance: your digital view from your computer or smart phone and the bank's view from the monthly bank statement. Internet banking is useful for tracking your bank balance in real time, but be aware that there can still be a timing difference, between the account value/balance you see online on your smart phone or computer compared to how much money is really in your bank account.

The timing difference occurs because there is a time delay from when you use a check or debit card or make a deposit to when the bank records/posts the transaction data. With check deposits, the deposit amount may or may not be immediately available for you to spend because the check amount must be actually paid to your bank by the bank from which it is written—called "clearing a check". These unrecorded transactions are called "outstanding items."

The delay in recording outstanding items can all cause your bank account to be temporarily overdrawn/out of money. This typically happens when people use checks, debit & ATM cards and recent deposit amounts to spend money falsely assuming that the bank balance they see online on their smart phone or computer is accurate.

Since banks charge extra fees for overdrawn transactions, it is important to keep track of all outstanding checking or debit card transactions until you see them reflected in your bank balance. You can do this by simply writing the amount on a "post it" note and posting on the BANK nail on your Budget Board. This will help keep from spending money that you have already spent.

In order to know exactly how much money you have in the bank, each month you must compare your online bank balance with the monthly bank statement for accuracy by making sure that all old and new transactions are reflected on both views. Any outstanding deposit transactions must be added and checks, debit card and ATM withdrawals subtracted from your bank statement. After all adjustments, you adjusted bank statement balance should equal your current digital bank balance (or your manual check register if you use one).

Regardless of what your definition of "financial success" looks like, budgeting is the first and most important step to achieving that definition. It will take time and effort to "live a budget"? Of course it will, but it's an investment in your financial well-being which is more than just worth it. The sense of financial self-reliance, which the sound money habit of budgeting can create, will enable you to make the most of your lifetime of financial challenges and opportunities. The sky is the limit and your budget is the launching pad!

Your budget will serve as your structured, yet flexible spending plan, based upon discretion and discipline. It will help you to use the power of "spend less than you earn" to generate a continuous cash flow of MAW dollars for building wealth.

Now it's time to reap the rewards of the sound money habit of Smart Spending ($+S^2$)—on to the SAVE pocket!

Think About It...

1. What would Shakespeare say if he were an economist?
2. Design your monthly budget using the worksheet example.
3. Which of the three Money Rules make budgeting so important?

6. The Save Pocket

Here Comes MAW

The SAVE pocket is the first stop for the MAW dollars created by Smart Spending (+S^2) in your SPEND pocket. Spending less of your PAW dollars than you earn generates excess PAW dollars which you can use as MAW dollars for saving and investing. This effectively converts excess PAW dollars to MAW dollars. These MAW dollars are your reward for sticking to your budget.

Once your MAW dollars are safely across the chasm, they serve their first two important purposes in your SAVE pocket.

The first purpose is to provide a lifestyle safety net for unexpected expenses such as a car repair or health emergency. These MAW dollars are called "emergency reserves."

Emergency reserves differ from expense reserves. Expense reserves are stored in a checking account to pay upcoming expenses which you know are not paid monthly, but are instead due every 60 or 90 days such as media subscriptions or utility bills. Emergency reserves are stored in a savings account and used to pay unexpected living expenses such as a car repair or health emergency.

The second purpose is funding short-term financial goals. These are goals with a duration of less than five years, such as education, travel and special projects. The MAW dollars used to fund them are simply called "savings."

Once you have fully funded these two savings purposes, any of your additional MAW dollars can be put to work in the INVEST pocket.

Save = Safe

This is the basic SAVE pocket formula, and like the budget formula from the SPEND pocket, it is obviously not math. Since the money in your SAVE pocket is intended to establish your safe foothold, it is called "safe money."

Safe money is essentially what its name suggests, but it has three aspects to its definition—location, risk and liquidity.

Location has two dimensions: institution—the financial institution where you deposit your MAW money; and account—a record of how much you have deposited with the institution.

On the Money Ride, institution means "bank." Banks, credit unions and savings & loans are all considered banks.

Think of an "account" as your personal bag of money at the bank. The bank calls the money in your savings account your "principal." There are different types of bags with different features. You will be able to choose, according to your saving objective, which type of bag(s) you use to store the money in your account.

Risk is the chance that you may lose money. In the SAVE pocket, risk is to be avoided at all times. A loss can result from downward fluctuations in the economy, financial markets or the value of a specific account. You will learn later in this section about how your SAVE pocket money can be protected from risk.

Liquidity is the ease with which your MAW money principal can be converted to cash on demand. Liquidity is an important consideration with every SAVE pocket account you establish. You want to be able to get cash when you need it.

The "Save = Safe" formula is a reminder, telling you to look for safety and liquidity when you stash your MAW dollars in your SAVE pocket. Just remember that with every MAW dollar in your SAVE pocket, safety is the first requirement.

As with every pocket on your Opportunity Vest, the dollars you stash in your SAVE pocket will require you to choose and decide. There are three basic questions you will have to answer with the MAW dollars you'll be vesting in your SAVE pocket:

1. How much?
2. How soon/How long?
3. Where?

These questions are interdependent, and the answers will change with your circumstances as you travel along on the Money Ride.

How Much?

"How much?" is the first and most important question you must answer with your MAW dollars in the SAVE pocket. Because it is the most important question, it is sometimes also the most challenging. This is because "How much?" must also take into account "How soon/How long?" your SAVE pocket dollars may be needed.

In order to form sound money habits in your SAVE pocket, it is important to treat saving money each month as though it were an expense. This means designating an amount for savings in your budget each month to maintain a flow of excess PAW dollars that can be converted to MAW dollars for saving and investing.

The amount you choose as your SAVE pocket target will depend upon the amount of PAW money you grab, the cost of your lifestyle and the amount of money you will need to fulfill your goals.

A good first target for lifestyle reserves would be an amount equal to your total living expenses for one month. The next reserves target would be three months' expenses. Your final reserves target would be six to twelve months' expenses.

As an example, let's say that you allocate at least 10% each month of your PAW dollars to your "MAW dollar expense." After ten months of budgeting you would then have the equivalent of one month's total income stashed in your SAVE pocket.

Once you have figured out the reserves amount, you'll then decide how much money you need for goals. While you will have short-term and long-term goals, only money for short-term goals is stashed in the SAVE pocket. You will learn about stashing money for long-term goals later in the INVEST pocket.

The price and the completion schedule for each goal will dictate the total amount you will need to have stored in your SAVE pocket.

First you will have to determine the amount of money needed for each goal. Then, based on when the goal must be completed, you must establish an objective for how much you need to save each

TMR Passenger Tips & Tools #9

What's Your Savings Target?

Think of savings as paying yourself first...setting money aside for you before you spend your first dollar each month.

What percentage of your take-home pay should you save each month? 10% is a good beginning target amount for establishing a sound money habit of saving.

But if you want to stay ahead of taxes, inflation and the other economic factors that can cause your money supply to decay, 20% of take-home pay should be your savings goal.

month to reach the goal on time. This is determined by your answer to the "How Soon" question which follows.

As with saving for emergency reserves, your target amount for all short-term goals should be part of your MAW dollars expense in your monthly budget. This will ensure that sufficient PAW dollars are converted to MAW dollars every month to cover the cost of your short-term goals.

Now that you know how to answer the "How much?" question, you're ready to move on to the next SAVE pocket question: "How soon/How long?"

How Soon/How Long?

After "How much?" comes the "How soon/How long?" question. The first part of the question deals with the liquid aspect of your SAVE pocket money: How soon do you need it, and how quickly can it be converted to cash?

How soon might you need to rely on your SAVE pocket reserves to help you through a financial emergency or take advantage of a financial opportunity? The timing is as impossible to predict as the amount, which makes having liquid dollars so essential.

This is why it is so important to start stashing dollars in your SAVE pocket as soon and as regularly as possible.

Now that you realize that you might need to depend on your

savings at any moment, the next question is how long might you need to rely on your savings to replace or supplement your monthly income?

What if you wanted to take advantage of a life opportunity which required that you move to a different city, state or country? How much would it cost to relocate, start your new life and live until your first paycheck arrives?

What about emergencies? What if because of an illness or injury you couldn't work for a while? How many months of living expenses might you need until you recover?

Finally, what about your life goals, like education, buying a home or a car, starting a new job or changing careers? These represent a potential need for MAW dollars to satisfy a short-term goal.

Regardless of the need or timing, the "How soon/How long?" question helps determine the savings goal and the deposits needed to reach it.

Now on to the last SAVE pocket question—"Where?"

Where?

The best place to put the MAW dollars you stash in your SAVE pocket is in a bank.

Banks may differ in name or type, but they all perform three basic functions—storing money, processing money and lending money. They provide storing and lending services by taking in deposits from customers and making loans to customers. Banks are authorized to lend a specified amount of money, which is based on the value of the bank's total deposits. Banks thus need deposits to make loans.

Banks attract deposits by offering you a fee to store your MAW dollars there. This fee is called "interest" and it is measured in percentages called "interest rates." The bank pays you interest based on your *principal* and the *holding period.* Principal is the amount of money you have in a savings account and the holding period is the length of time your money remains in a savings account.

Interest is typically calculated using a special type of math formula called "compounding." With compounding, the interest your account earns is calculated based on your original deposit plus any interest earned in prior periods. The interest you earn each period is added to your account value and included in the next interest calculation.

Compound interest is calculated periodically where the interest rate for each period represents a fraction of the annual rate based on how many times each year it is calculated. The most common periods used for calculating compound interest are: daily (1/365), monthly (1/12) and quarterly (1/4).

Banks can choose the interest rates they use for calculating interest, but they typically use the interest rates set by the Federal Reserve System (Fed), a government agency, as a base rate for setting rates they pay on savings accounts. The Fed changes rates periodically in attempts to control the rate of inflation in the economy. When the inflation rate increases, interest rates trend higher; and when the inflation rate decreases, interest rates trend lower.

The advantage of compounding is that you not only earn interest

TMR Passenger Tips & Tools #10

Compounding Formula:

$$FV = P(1+r/n)^{nt}$$

The compounding formula is also known as the "Time Value of Money Formula."

FV = Future value
P = Present value/principal
r/n = Interest rate
nt = Number of time periods

Using this formula, if you deposited $100 MAW dollars in a savings account at 5% interest compounded monthly for ten years, your MAW dollars in the account would grow to $164.89.

$$FV = 100(1+(5/12))^{12 \times 5}$$
$$FV = \$164.89$$

TMR Passenger Tips & Tools #11

The Rule of 72

If you want to know how long it will take for compounding to double the value of your MAW dollars, divide "72" by the interest rate your money will earn.

Example: If the bank offers to pay you 7.2% interest annually on your principal, it will take how many years for your money to double in value?

$$72 \div 7.2 = 10$$

It will take ten years for your principal to double if you earn 7.2% interest each year.

on your principal, you also earn interest on the interest you earned in prior periods—this is compounding in action. Compounding is the ripple effect of saving, and this is why your SAVE pocket money qualifies as MAW, (Money at Work.)

In addition to compounding, there is a second type of interest formula that you should be aware of, called "simple interest." This type of interest is rarely used, but it deserves mention so that you are able to make smart SAVE pocket money decisions if you are offered this option.

Simple interest is, as its name suggests, simple. Unlike compounding, simple interest is paid each period on the principal only. There is no interest paid on the interest received in prior periods.

While compound and simple interest produce different results, they share a common dynamic—the higher the interest rate, the faster your MAW dollars grow each year.

Interest rates are important, but they are not the only factor to consider in selecting a financial institution. Another important consideration is the type of account in which you choose to store your SAVE pocket money.

Your answer to the "How soon/How long?" question will suggest the best type of savings account to use. In the SAVE pocket,

TMR Passenger Tips & Tools #12

Simple Interest Formula:

FV = P (1+rt)

From the prior example you know that $100 will grow to $162.89 in ten years at 5% using compounding.

If you use the simple interest formula to calculate the interest earned at 5%, you would end up with $150.00 after ten years.

The longer the period or higher the interest, the greater the difference in ending value would be.

FV = P (1+rt)
FV = 100 (1 + (.05 x 10)
FV = 100 (1.5)
FV = $150

"How soon?" indicates how soon you may need to take the money out of savings for an emergency or goal. "How long?" indicates how long the money must last once you take it out of savings for a particular emergency or goal. Will it require only a single withdrawal from your savings for a car repair or will it require ongoing monthly withdrawals to cover education expenses?

There are three standard types of savings accounts: (1) personal savings account; (2) money market savings account; and (3) certificate of deposit. Generally, you could use any of the three for both short-term and long-term savings goals. However, each account type has specific features that can make it the best option for a particular situation. Account features define how much you must deposit, the interest rate you earn, and any time limits or penalties for withdrawing money from your savings (liquidity).

Here are the standard account features for each savings account type.

Personal Savings Account

A basic savings account is very safe because it is insured by the Federal Deposit Insurance Corporation (FDIC) up to $250,000 per person, per bank. The required minimum deposit and balance to open and maintain an account is typically $25. This type of account is very *liquid*, which means there is no time limit or penalty for withdrawals; you have immediate access to your money when you need it. The interest earned is typically compounded daily. Because the liquidity is not limited, the annual interest rate on personal savings accounts is very low compared to other savings vehicles which limit your liquidity access. A personal savings account is a good choice for short-term emergency reserves and goals where safety of principal an unlimited liquidity are most important.

Money Market Savings Account

This type of savings account issued by banks, insured by the FDIC, offers variable interest rates and usually earns a higher rate of interest than a basic savings account. There are, however, *trade-offs* for that higher interest rate: higher deposit minimums and limits on withdrawals. This type of savings account requires minimum deposits of $500 to $1,000, and limits withdrawals to three to six times annually. Interest is compounded daily, and the annual rate will vary because banks like to offer competitive rates on money market accounts to attract customers.

This type of account is a good choice for short-term (less than 1 year) saving, if the limits on withdrawals will not cause a future cash-flow problem. It will also work for long-term saving (less than five years), since more frequent withdrawals are possible than from a CD.

Certificate of Deposit (CD)

This type of savings vehicle can be used for holding periods of one, three, and six months, and one to four years. CDs are what's called a *time deposit*, since you agree not to withdraw your money until a specific ending date, called the *maturity date*. CDs are insured by the FDIC, and can earn higher interest rates than basic savings accounts and money market accounts. The interest rate on a CD is fixed during the holding period. The liquidity of CDs is limited by the maturity date, and you will pay a penalty for early withdrawals in the form of forfeiting interest you would have earned.

This type of savings account can be used for short-term (less than 1 year) or long-term (less than 5 years) saving, as long as the CD's maturity date doesn't create a situation where an early withdrawal becomes necessary.

It is important to realize that, excluding deposits, not much wealth building will take place in your SAVE pocket because of the relationship between time and money. The MAW dollars stored in your SAVE pocket will be there for a limited amount of time. Interest earned is the product of principal, the rate and the number of periods it is earned. SAVE pocket dollars usually don't generate a lot of interest earnings because the interest rate is typically too low and earnings period too short to take full advantage of long-term compound interest.

Real wealth-building, based on time and money, happens in your INVEST pocket, where you will learn to work with larger amounts of MAW dollars over longer periods of time.

So, the sooner you stash the appropriate amount of MAW dollars in your SAVE pocket, the sooner you can move on to the challenges, excitement and rewards waiting for you in the INVEST pocket.

No time to waste—on to the INVEST pocket!

Think About It...

1. How does a PAW dollar get converted to a MAW dollar?
2. What short-term (less than 5 years) goal would you like to save for?
3. What kind of bank savings account might currently work best for you?

7. The Invest Pocket

MAW Goes to Work

The INVEST pocket is where your ability to exercise budget Discretion & Discipline (D^2) to generate excess PAW dollars in your SPEND pocket and convert them to MAW dollars for investing. This is where your MAW dollars apply their real wealth-building muscle.

Once you begin stashing MAW dollars in your INVEST pocket, the focus of your Money I.Q. shifts from Smart Spending and saving to making the most of investment opportunities to build wealth.

> **TMR Passenger Tips & Tools #13**
>
> **Successful Investing Takes a Lot of D^2**
>
> Before you invest, remember how hard you had to work to grab your PAW dollars and how much D^2 it took to create your first MAW dollars.
>
> You will need an equal amount of discretion and discipline to design an effective investment strategy and stay with it for the long run. So, respect your MAW dollars for the hard work and D^2 they represent by always being vigilant and diligent in managing your investments.

The opportunities will be many and varied, and your financial success will depend on your ability to make informed choices. This means you need to know *what* you are doing, *how* it works and *where* it fits in relation to your other financial goals and objectives.

Before we get into the specifics of how the INVEST pocket works, it's important that you have an understanding about the INVEST pocket's fundamental purpose: wealth—what it is and what it means to you.

Wealth

On the Money Ride there are two kinds of wealth: financial wealth and personal wealth.

Financial wealth is the market value of assets and the income generated by assets. The income provides cash flow to live on. The market value reflects an asset's current price and its potential for future growth. Financial wealth is money at work (MAW) in your INVEST pocket. The MAW dollars are invested to grow asset value and to generate income.

When you retire and you're no longer grabbing PAW dollars, your wealth assets must generate MAW income to replace the PAW income. Your MAW income is generated directly by an asset such as rental income, interest income, stock dividends etc. This MAW income is called "passive income" because you don't have to actively grab these dollars as you do with PAW dollars. Passive income is the Today Dollar value of your INVEST pocket income.

In addition to the MAW income, the potential future increase in the market value of your assets offers the potential for increased future income. This increase in future value and income helps insulate your wealth and cash flow against the eroding effects of inflation,

TMR Passenger Tips & Tools #14

The Tomorrow Dollar Value of Your Money

Every Today Dollar, represented by PAW and MAW dollars in your money supply, has the potential to grow if you hang on to it and efficiently put it to work. This is the Tomorrow Dollar value of your money—its potential to build wealth in the form of assets which generate income and/or grow in value.

Remember...attitudes and values about wealth are personal, but the money rules and mechanics for building wealth are the same for everyone.

The primary challenge of building wealth is balancing your consumption of Today Dollars with the need to create a supply of Tomorrow Dollars.

taxes and expenses. The potential to generate future income is the Tomorrow Dollar value of the wealth you create with your INVEST pocket dollars.

On the Money Ride, the whole point of pursuing financial success and wealth is to live a happier, more fulfilled life. This is personal wealth, and your definition of personal wealth as important as your definition of financial wealth.

Personal wealth includes aspects of your life where it is not money itself that is important, but rather the abundance of people, experiences and opportunities that you enjoy. These may include values like supporting a family, reaching personal growth goals and helping others in need.

Your personal definition influences the lifestyle you *want* to live, which in turn determines the amount of money you'll *need* to live.

Your working definition of wealth will help you focus on your INVEST pocket goals and monitor your wealth-building progress.

There are four dynamics at work in the INVEST pocket which make it very different from the SAVE pocket: risk, reward, growth and income. These are the roller coaster "ups and downs" of building wealth.

Invest = Risk

You'll remember that the primary characteristic of the MAW dollars stashed in your SAVE pocket is that they are safe dollars (SAVE = Safe). This means that there is little or no danger in the SAVE pocket of losing your money.

In the INVEST pocket there is always risk—the possibility that you may lose some or all of the MAW dollars you stash there. Because of the constant presence of risk, it is impossible to accurately predict the future value of an investment—you can only *estimate* or *project* the future value. This is what makes INVEST pocket dollars fundamentally different from SAVE pocket dollars, which are exposed to little or no risk.

In order to successfully deal with risk, you must start by asking yourself two basic questions:

1. What is the type, degree and probability of risk for a particular investment?
2. What is my risk tolerance?

Answering these two questions involves some "figuring" and some "feeling."

The figuring part is doing your homework to determine what risks are present in a potential investment and how much risk you can afford to take. This will involve identifying the source of risk, how it might occur, how it might be offset or avoided and ultimately how much money it may cause you to lose. This research is an important aspect of your Money I.Q.

The feeling part is being honest with yourself about how the thought of losing your MAW dollars makes you feel. This is called your risk tolerance, and it is based upon how risk affects you emotionally and financially. Your tolerance of risk will be the dominant influence, both in terms of the amount you invest and the type of investment you choose. On the other hand, passengers who aren't comfortable with risk prefer more conservative investments. These are investments where there is little risk of losing MAW dollars. They are usually less likely to make a lot of money or make it as quickly as aggressive, high-risk investments. At times, the conservative passenger may feel more comfortable keeping more MAW dollars in the SAVE pocket rather than in the INVEST pocket.

So, ultimately your success in the INVEST pocket will come down to how many MAW dollars you have to invest, how many MAW dollars you want or need for future goals and what kind of Money Person you are when it comes to dealing with risk.

Figuring and feeling are both part of every investment decision you will make on the Money Ride. So, let's explore the figuring first, then we'll talk about the feeling part of the process.

What makes risk so interesting and challenging is that there are three basic types or elements of risk in every investment opportunity. Each represents a chance to make or lose precious MAW dollars, so pay attention to these when considering every investment opportunity.

The Three Levels of Risk

1. The Economy

This is the "big picture" level of risk. Both the general state of the economy and the major economic factors of interest rates, inflation and financial markets can have an impact on the performance of investments.

Generally, the performance of investments will reflect the performance of the overall economy. Interest rates, inflation rates and the financial markets serve as indicators of the health and direction of the economy and have their own particular impact on investment performance. For instance the combination of low interest rates and low inflation usually stimulate growth in the economy which in turn stimulates growth in the value of investment assets like stocks and real estate.

2. The Industry

The next level of risk research involves analyzing the industry in which the investment operates.

Is the investment in a profitable and stable industry?

Is it an emerging industry with a future, an established industry with a history, or a fading industry offering outmoded products or services?

Is there a current demand and/or future demand for the industry's goods and services?

Is the industry reliant on consumer spending or government spending?

These are the types of questions you need to explore when assessing the potential of investing in a particular industry.

3. Investment

Once you have completed your research on the risk implications of the economy and the industry involved, your last step is to analyze the risk attributed to a specific investment. This may involve investigating a company, a real estate property or an investment company that manages MAW dollars for investors.

Is it profitable, financially strong and well managed?

Is there demand for its products or services?

Is it known in its industry for some special feature or innovation?

The best candidates may not be obvious at first, but by asking the right questions, the investments with solid wealth-building potential will be easier to identify.

You'll have to do your INVEST pocket homework to learn as much as you can about every source of risk before you invest. Remember, on the Money Ride homework is fun and profitable. Smart, disciplined passengers get paid to do their INVEST pocket homework—with wealth!

Risk = Emotion

After you have done the figuring work of identifying the type and degree of risk, it's time to explore the feeling aspect of risk.

If you want to maximize the wealth potential of your INVEST pocket and enjoy life, it is important to feel comfortable with the degree of risk in your investments—remember your risk tolerance.

Most people are risk averse and tend to avoid risky investments. However, by understanding more about an investment, you can reduce your risk anxiety and be more confident and comfortable with more investment choices.

Now that you are aware of how risk influences your investment decisions, it's time for you to learn about the second unique INVEST pocket dynamic: Reward.

Invest = Reward

Your research on risk is never complete until it gives equal consideration to the dynamic of reward. Reward is the potential to make money on an investment, either from an increase in its market value (growth) or from the cash flow (income) it generates.

Risk and reward are the two sides of the investment decision coin. Since either side may result, the likelihood of each happening must be compared in order to make an informed investment decision.

You must research the potential reward of an investment offer just as thoroughly as you study its risk, so that you can gauge its probability as accurately as possible. Doing your homework on *both* sides of the investment decision scale will help you feel more comfortable with your investment choices.

Your understanding of the risk/reward relationship will help you intelligently expand your risk tolerance, regardless of what type of Money Person you are. This expanded tolerance will mean that more investment opportunities will qualify as appropriate choices for you.

Invest = Growth

The overall goal of every INVEST pocket decision is to build wealth through investing. Therefore, growth is the primary objective with every MAW dollar you stash in your INVEST pocket. The potential for growth is what you should look for in every investment opportunity that comes your way on the Money Ride. The key to your financial success will be using your Money I.Q. to transform growth potential into wealth measured in dollars.

In order to gauge your success at transforming growth potential into wealth, you first have to know how to measure growth and the wealth it produces. On the Money Ride, the wealth you create by investing MAW dollars is measured in the value of assets. An asset is defined as property you own which has two basic characteristics: the potential to grow in value and the potential to generate income.

Any increase in an asset's market value in excess of what you originally paid for it is money gained in growth. Growth can be converted to cash by selling an investment for a profit.

The key is to invest in assets which achieve growth that is continual and consistent. This sustained growth must also be at a pace or rate sufficient to stay ahead of the factors which erode money, such as taxes, inflation, fluctuating interest rates and market declines. Only by growth outpacing these eroding factors can real wealth be created.

Another important aspect of growth you must be aware of is the element of time. The value of some investments can increase very quickly. For instance, stock share prices can change dramatically in a matter of seconds or minutes. However, growth is typically not about getting rich quickly. While there are sophisticated and aggressive investing strategies offering the potential for large short-term gains, the fundamentals of growth are based on long-term participation in an investment.

Invest = Income

In addition to growth, the second valuable characteristic of investment assets is the capacity to generate income. Income is the cash generated by an investment. Income can be in the form of a dividend

TMR Passenger Tips & Tools #15

Automatic Investing

Time and discipline are important in successful investing. So start early and try making your investment contributions automatic to sustain a disciplined investing program...time will take care of the rest.

Research investment opportunities which allow you to electronically transfer MAW dollars from your bank account each month to your investment accounts.

as with stocks, interest as with bonds or rent as with real estate. The income objective typically takes a back seat to growth in the early stages of the wealth building process. However, as you reach the end of your PAW dollar–grabbing years, generating income from your MAW dollars will become the primary objective.

In order to meet this switch in emphasis from growth to income, you will have to reallocate a portion of your MAW dollars from assets that do not generate income to those that do. This means moving some of your MAW dollars into investments that generate interest, dividends, rents, etc.

Though the primary objective for your MAW dollars may shift to generating income, you will still want to have some of your MAW dollars invested for growth so that you will have sufficient assets to generate Tomorrow Dollars for future lifestyle income.

Next up, we will explore the process of investing so that you will be better equipped to evaluate the growth and income potential of an investment before you invest.

Investing Process

There are three fundamental ways to put MAW dollars to work in your INVEST pocket: Invest, Diversify and Reinvest. Regardless of which investments you choose for growing your MAW dollars, your decisions will involve one or more of these three key action steps.

Invest

This is the obvious purpose of your INVEST pocket. It represents the routine of regularly stashing MAW dollars in your INVEST pocket as investment capital to build wealth.

The regular, systematic stashing of MAW dollars in your INVEST pocket is a sound money habit which can generate the Tomorrow Dollars you'll need to reach long-term financial goals.

Diversify

Diversification is a valuable tool for dealing with investment risk and increasing wealth-building opportunity. If you simply accumulate all of your MAW dollars in a single investment, you will always be exposed to the same type and degree of risk. You will also be limiting yourself to only one asset category to build wealth. The single investment approach can work if you are lucky, but luck is not a reliable approach to dealing with risk or building an investment portfolio. Even if you decide to invest exclusively in a particular category of investment like real estate or stocks, it will still make sense to diversify your holdings in two or more investments within the same category.

Diversifying to mange risk involves investing in two or more investments with different risk characteristics. This approach will effectively spread your exposure to risk over the different investments, rather than concentrating all of your risk exposure in a single investment. Keep in mind that diversification does not totally eliminate risk.

Reinvest

Like a farmer harvesting corn, you will be harvesting your crop of new MAW dollars which grow from the seeds of your original MAW investment capital and using it as seed to grow additional wealth.

Investments can generate new MAW capital from increased market value and/or income that it pays such as dividend and interest income. You will first have to pay a tax on the profit you earn

TMR Passenger Tips & Tools #16

Reinvesting Your MAW Profits

If you invest $1,000 to buy 100 shares of stock for $10/share and 10 years later its market value increases to $20/share, the increase represents a profit of $1,000.

You could then sell 50 shares for $20/share, generating $1,000 in cash including $500 in profit...pay tax of approximately $100, and have $900 left to reinvest.

You would end up with your original $1,000 still invested in 50 shares and an additional $900 to reinvest in a new investment to diversify your portfolio.

from selling the asset and will then have the net after-tax amount available to invest.

When using increased market value for reinvestment, you sell a portion of your investment representing profit and invest it in something different from the original investment. For example, you could take the profit earned on your stock portfolio and use it to invest in real estate or another alternative investment.

If an investment generates income and you want to invest more in the original investment, you can have the income automatically used to reinvest. For example, if you own company stock which pays dividends to investors, you can use the dividend you receive to purchase additional shares of the same stock. In many cases, you can set up an investment to have income reinvested automatically to purchase more of the same investment.

Whether from growth in market value or income, reinvesting profits builds wealth by either increasing the value or number of assets you own. Each new asset represents an additional opportunity to build wealth through growth and/or income. Intelligent reinvesting allows you to keep your MAW dollars working at optimum wealth-building capacity.

Investing wisely requires an investment strategy suited to your objectives and resources—your goals and your supply of MAW dollars. To develop your strategy, you can start by asking yourself the same three basic questions you used in the SAVE pocket: How much?, How soon/How long? and Where?

How Much?

Just as with the SAVE pocket, "How much?" is the first and most important question you must answer with your MAW dollars in the INVEST pocket...with one difference. In the INVEST pocket, "How much?" is a two-part question. The first question is, "How much MAW capital do you have to invest?" The second question is, "How much in Today Dollars do you need for a particular life goal or objective?"

The first answer is the amount of MAW capital you have available to invest will be a function of your ability to sustain the sound money habit of budgeting to generate excess PAW dollars which can then be converted to MAW capital.

The second answer involves estimating the future expense or value of a long-term goal. Start with identifying the current cost or value of the long-term goal event or item. Because most expenses and values typically increase over time due to inflation and other economic influences, these must be considered for a more realistic estimate.

For your estimate you can use past expense and value history of the event or item. If no history is available, you can use a financial calculator (available free online) to estimate the future expense or value assuming various inflation rates for the time frame that matches your long-term goal completion date. For example, if the cost of four years of college tuition costs $100,000 today, at 3% annual inflation for 18 years is estimated to be $170,243.

Part of calculating "how much" you need to reach a long-term goal is figuring "how soon" you will need to start using the Tomorrow Dollars accumulated in an investment. You also need to figure, once you start spending the Tomorrow Dollars, "how long" you need the money to last for completion of the long-term goal. Now let's look at the How Soon/How Long question.

Passengers on the Money Ride who don't mind risk tend to prefer more high-risk investments. These are investments which offer the potential to either make a lot of money or lose a lot of money. They may also offer quick profits, as opposed to slow and steady long-term growth of MAW dollars.

How Soon/How Long?

The INVEST pocket is typically used only for generating money for long-term life goals. These are goals which will take five years or longer to reach.

An important objective of the investing process is finding investments with a timetable that is compatible with the timetable of a particular financial goal.

The timetable of an investment is called its holding period—how long you plan to own the investment before hopefully selling it for a profit and converting it to cash. Ideally, the holding period of an investment will suit the timetable of a particular goal. This timing will rarely be perfect, but it is still sound planning to match the holding period in your investment choices with your goal timetables.

Once you have invested the MAW dollars that will eventually fund a goal, you must monitor the investment's performance regularly—monthly, quarterly, annually—to keep the timetable of the investment and the goal in step. If your investing activity involves frequent buying and selling or if you are within two years of a goal completion target date, you should check your investment performance ever quarter or month. If your investing is less frequent such as annually and your are at least three years from your goal target date, monitoring your investments on an annual or semi-annual basis may be sufficient.

Now that you are aware of the influence of timing on your INVEST pocket decisions, you're ready to deal with the final INVEST pocket question—"Where?"

Where?

There are investment opportunities waiting for you at every twist and turn on the Money Ride. The number and variety of choices may seem overwhelming at times, but all investment opportunities will fall into one of six basic categories: business ownership, stocks, bonds, real estate, commodities and collectibles.

Business Ownership

Business ownership means owning your own business, either by yourself or with one or more partners. Any company which is owned by a limited number of individuals where the ownership opportunity is not available to the general public is a "privately held" company.

The incentive for being a business owner is the opportunity to create wealth by growing the value of your business. The value of your business will be based upon its capacity to generate a profit by having more cash flow coming in as income than you have cash flow going out as expenses. The higher your profits, the higher the value of your business.

On the Money Ride, profitable businesses are called "right side up" businesses and unprofitable businesses are called "upside down" businesses.

In an ideal world, your business would be "right side up" all the time, but this is tough to accomplish. In fact, most businesses experience times when they are not generating profits, especially when they are first getting started.

In order to survive and prosper, the unprofitable times must be seldom and brief—on the Money Ride you don't want to get stuck "upside down." As long as your business is operating "right side up," you're earning an income and building wealth.

In addition to earning an income and building wealth, there are other benefits to owning your own business. As the owner of a company you get to work for yourself. You are your own boss.

As your own boss you have more freedom to do the work you want to do and work the way you want. But with the freedom also comes responsibility and risk—the responsibility of making all the

TMR Passenger Tips & Tools #17

Want to Be an Entrepreneur?

Entrepreneurs play an important role in our society and economy. They are the people who are willing to risk everything they own to create a business, and if they are successful they reap the rewards they deserve.

So, if you want to be one, first go work for one and learn by first being a productive employee. Show initiative, ask questions, watch and learn...it's how many successful business owners start—as a hard-working, productive employee.

key decisions and the risk of possibly losing everything you have invested in the business.

Regardless of whether it offers a product or service, every business operates in its customers' SPEND pocket. As your customers buy your products or services, their SPEND dollars represent revenue to your business. Every revenue dollar you don't spend on the expenses of running your company is a dollar of profit.

As the owner, you can either take profit dollars as personal income or reinvest profit dollars to grow your business. As your business grows, if you manage it well its profits can continue to increase. As profits increase, the value of your business increases—this is how a business owner creates wealth.

Stocks

Stocks and bonds are the most common investments for employing the accumulation approach to building wealth. However, stocks and bonds are different in what they do and how they do it.

A stock represents a proportional share of ownership in a company organized as a corporation. Corporations can be private or public companies.

Private companies are corporations which usually have a small number of shareholders; the shares are bought and sold privately among individuals. Private corporations are also called "privately-held companies."

Public companies are corporations which usually have large numbers of shares owned by the investing public called "outstanding shares." Their shares are typically bought and sold on a public markets called the stock market, through "securities exchanges." Buy-and-sell stock trades are transacted through financial companies known as "securities dealers." Investment firms, banks, insurance companies and financial planning firms typically have a relationship with a securities dealer so that their representatives can sell stocks and other investments to the public.

When you own a company's stock, you own a certain amount of the company's outstanding shares, whose value is the market price of a share. As a shareholder, you often have the right to vote on decisions about how the company is run. You also share in the profits and losses of the company. When the share price goes up the value of your investment goes up, and when the share price drops your investment loses value.

The degree of change in a stock's price is called "volatility." A stock whose price change is greater in degree than the change in the overall market is said to be volatile. Regardless of the degree of volatility, these increases and decreases in price and value present opportunity and challenges for investing your MAW dollars in stocks.

In addition to increasing share price, stocks can contribute to wealth-building a second way. Some companies distribute a portion of profits to the shareholders in cash payments called "dividends." Dividends are typically paid annually or quarterly. As a shareholder you have the option to either take the dividend as cash or use it to buy more shares in the company for future growth.

Regardless of whether you invest in stocks for growth or income, you need to have an organized approach to selecting stocks. A selection of stocks is called a stock portfolio and should contain a variety of different types of companies with different growth and risk potential.

Stocks can be grouped into three basic classes, based on company size: large capital, medium capital and small capital. The "capital" stands for the amount of money a company has. Size is important because it is related to the growth and risk potential of a company.

Small companies typically offer the greatest growth upside and risk downside. Small companies have a lot of potential to grow, but they also represent significant risk because they have less capital to weather hard times and stay competitive. This means that you can expect the share price of your small company stocks to experience greater price volatility than the shares of larger companies. Small company stocks will definitely add some excitement to your Money Ride adventure.

Medium-size companies offer a more moderate degree of growth and risk potential than smaller companies. They may also offer the potential for dividend income. The shares you own in medium-size companies are the middle ground of your diversified portfolio. They offer less risk potential than small company stocks, along with greater growth potential than large company stocks.

Large companies offer less growth potential, less risk and greater long-term stability than small- and medium-size companies. They also offer more potential for dividend income. Your large company stocks will serve as the stable, long-term foundation of your portfolio.

Bonds

Bonds are different from stocks, both in how they work and in the role they play in your INVEST pocket.

Like stocks, bonds are bought and sold in the financial markets through securities firms. Bonds are generally considered to have less risk than stocks and are used primarily for safety and income. When corporations and government entities need additional capital for general use or specific projects, they raise the money by issuing bonds which they sell to the public. Owning a bond is like owning an IOU for the money you lend to the issuing entity.

A bond is a promise by the issuing entity to repay the amount borrowed and to pay the bond holder interest for the use of the money. The interest payments are typically paid to the bond holder every six months.

The promise to repay is backed either by the financial strength of the issuing entity or by the income generated by the specific use of the bond proceeds, such as building toll roads and bridges. This financial backing is the bondholder's assurance that the interest will be paid and the debt repaid. If the issuing entity is unable to pay interest or repay the debt, the bondholder has a right to receive repayment from the financial assets of the entity. This financial backing is what gives a bond an added degree of safety over other investments.

A bond works much like a CD except that the term of a bond is longer and the interest paid is usually higher. The term of a bond typically ranges from ten to thirty years, depending upon whether the bond issuer is a company or government entity.

The beginning of the bond term is called the "issue date" and the end of the bond term is called the "maturity date." The bondholder receives interest payments during the bond term based on the bond's fixed interest rate, called the "coupon rate." For bonds with a term longer than one year, the interest payments are typically made every six months. A bond must be repaid no later than its maturity date. However, a bond may be repaid sooner by the issuing entity if the bond agreement allows.

The interest paid on bonds issued by corporations and the federal government is taxed just like your paycheck, as ordinary income. However, interest paid on bonds issued by city, county and state governments is federal tax-free and state tax-free if you live in the state in which the bond is issued.

A bond's price moves up and down with the prevailing market interest rates. When the prevailing market interest rate rises above a bond's coupon rate, the bond's price drops. When the prevailing market interest drops below the coupon rate, the bond's price rises. You can sell a bond at any time prior to the maturity date to either raise cash or earn a profit by selling at a higher price.

If you hold a bond until its maturity date, the loan is repaid and

TMR Passenger Tips & Tools #18

Loaner vs. Owner

Remember that you do not invest in bonds for growth. With bonds you are a "loaner" not an "owner." When a bond matures, your original principal is returned to you...before the maturity date you only receive simple interest on your principal, no real growth.

Bonds have an important role in an investment portfolio, but safety and income is what they are used for, not growth.

you get your original investment back. This means that you received interest income during the bond term, but you do not realize any growth on your original investment.

So, if you purchase a stock you are an "owner" and if you purchase a bond you are a "loaner." Owners take more risks and are ultimately concerned with a "return *on* their principal." Loaners, on the other hand, take little or no risk in return for a stable income flow and are ultimately more concerned with the "return *of* their principal."

Now that you know the basics of investing in individual stocks and bonds, it's a good time to learn about an alternative way to build a stock and bond portfolio—mutual funds.

Mutual Funds

It is important to understand that mutual funds are not a separate type of investment like stocks, bonds and real estate, they are instead what is called an "investment structure." Like a can of mixed nuts, they are a method of packaging an investment product for sale to the public. The package is the mutual fund, and the contents are usually portfolios of stocks and/or bonds.

Mutual funds are the most popular way to invest in stocks and bonds. You will find that over half of the passengers you meet on the Money Ride invest in mutual funds.

TMR Passenger Tips & Tools #19

Picking a Mutual Fund

Don't chase short-term performance records...look for a fund with a leading long-term performance history.

Look for fund managers who have been with a fund for a long time.

Compare fund expenses and fees...both decrease a fund's gains.

Match the fund's investment objective and risk/reward potential with your investment objectives and risk tolerance.

There are two basic advantages to using mutual funds in your INVEST pocket—diversification and professional management.

Mutual funds operate on the basic principle of diversification. A mutual fund is an investment company which collects MAW dollars from the public and invests the pool of money in stocks and/or bonds. The large pool of money enables the investment company to purchase thousands of shares of hundreds of companies, creating a much larger portfolio than you can as an individual. This allows you to participate in a well-diversified portfolio which spreads risk and expands the opportunity for growth.

Mutual funds employ investment experts who create and manage this large portfolio of individual stocks and bonds on your behalf. The investment management team makes buy-and-sell decisions for you, taking the guesswork out of your stock and bond investment choices.

The mutual fund charges a fee for managing the fund's portfolio. The fee is based on a percentage of the fund's total value and is deducted periodically from the fund's earnings or assets.

When you invest in a mutual fund, you purchase shares in the fund rather than shares of individual stocks or bonds. Mutual fund shares are either purchased and redeemed directly with the mutual fund company or through a stock exchange using a brokerage account.

Every mutual fund has a particular investment objective, which can be defined by the kind of stocks and bonds it owns or by its investment style. The terms "large cap," "international" and "S&P 500 index" are examples of mutual funds defined by what they own. The terms "growth," "value" and "aggressive growth" are examples of mutual funds defined by their management style.

Mutual funds take the guesswork out of picking individual stocks and bonds, but you will still have some homework to do in choosing a mutual fund. You will have thousands of mutual funds to choose from on the Money Ride, and you must base your choices on the funds' objectives, investment styles, management fees and long-term performance record.

Real Estate

Real estate is usually a long-term investment, which offers the potential for income and growth. Real estate generates income by charging people rent to use the property. The growth comes from the increase in the market price of a property.

The income and growth potential of real estate is primarily determined by its location. Depending upon its intended use, you want to invest in a property that is located where people want to live, work or play. The current and future economic prospects for the area are also an important consideration.

There are three basic types of real estate. The first type is land, which is property that does not have any buildings on it. The second type is residential real estate, which is property with buildings where people live. The third type is commercial real estate, which is land with buildings where people work.

When investing in land, the goal is either to hold the land for resale or to build something on it. Holding it for resale usually means owning a property for a longer period of time. The hope is that eventually the property's location will attract a buyer who is willing to pay a higher price than you paid for it.

Land can also be purchased with the plan to build a residential or commercial building on the property. The process of buying land

and then constructing a building on it is called "developing" and people who do it are called "developers."

As a developer, your goal is to ultimately sell a property for a profit or keep it for its rental income and growth potential.

The more common INVEST pocket opportunity in real estate is to buy an existing residential or commercial property. With an existing property, the initial goal is to generate enough rental income to pay expenses and generate a profit.

Regardless of the type of property you decide to buy on the Money Ride, real estate has an advantage over other investments in how it can be purchased.

Other Peoples' Money

When you buy real estate, the money you pay for it does not all have to be yours. You actually get to use "other peoples' money"—OPM—to pay part of the purchase price of a property. The other great thing about it is that your part of the total price can be a lot smaller than the OPM part. So, where does the OPM come from?

OPM is a general term for a loan or debt. OPM can come from individuals or financial institutions. The type of debt used to purchase real estate is called a "mortgage loan." You can use a mortgage to buy your personal residence or to buy a residential or commercial rental property which generates income.

You can pay 80% of the purchase price of real estate using a mortgage; 20% you pay in cash as a "down payment." So, you can "buy" a $250,000 real property for a $50,000 down payment out of your pocket combined with an $200,000 mortgage loan. The mortgage will take 30 years to pay off. You start out as a 20% owner with a bank as your partner who owns 80%. All you have to do is make the payments for 30 years, and you will be a 100% owner.

When it comes to reinvesting, real estate has a unique advantage over the other types of investments. With most investments, in order to reinvest cash from profits, you must first pay tax on the profits when you sell the investment to raise cash.

With real estate you can actually take the profit out of a prop-

TMR Passenger Tips & Tools #20

The Real Estate Advantage

Franklin Frugal and Freddy Flash together purchased a rental house for $250,000 using a cash down payment of $50,000 and a mortgage loan from a bank of $200,000.

Years later the market value of the property had grown to $400,000 and the remaining principal owed on the mortgage was $100,000. Franklin and Freddy decided they wanted to use some of the increased value of the property to buy another house for $500,000 to expand their real estate empire...refinancing was the answer and here is how it worked.

They they needed $100,000 for a down payment and a mortgage loan of $400,000 to buy the new property. So, the refinance of the original property would consist of a new mortgage of $200,000 to pay off the existing mortgage of $100,000 and take $100,000 in profit (new MAW dollars) for the cash down payment to purchase the new property.

Franklin and Freddy now own two houses worth a total of $900,000 with total mortgage debt of $600,000 for a net equity value of $300,000...all made possible by an initial cash investment of $50,000 on the first house.

erty in order to buy another property, without having to sell the first property. You also don't have to pay tax on the profit until you ultimately sell the property. This is accomplished by using a strategy called refinancing.

Refinancing is a method of replacing the loan (mortgage) originally used to purchase the property a new loan. The amount borrowed on the new mortgage loan would be enough to pay off the balance owed on the original loan plus the profit available to use to buy a new property.

This strategy allows you to take the profit from a property and use it to buy a second property and do it without having to pay tax on the profit until you eventually sell the property—see Passenger Tips & Tools #20, above, for an example.

The opportunity to use refinancing, take profits without paying current taxes, gives real estate a special advantage when it comes to reinvesting.

Keep in mind that the values, prices, interest rates and percentage of OPM will change, depending on the economy. However, the basic approach to building wealth in real estate is real and always available in your INVEST pocket when the right opportunity presents itself.

Commodities

A commodity is largely nature's contribution to the world of investments. Most commodities are agricultural product like corn, pigs and orange juice or a raw material like coal, gold and oil. Currency, though obviously not an agricultural product, is also considered a commodity because its value fluctuates like that of a commodity.

Regardless of the type, the prices of all commodities fluctuate based on supply and demand...how many people need or want it (demand) and how much of it is available to buy (supply).

Commodities are growth investments, not income investments. People invest in commodities based on the belief that their price will increase because of a change in supply and demand. This is obviously the same basic reason that people invest in stocks, real estate and businesses. However, since nature has a more direct influence on a commodity's supply and demand than it has on other types of investments, investing in commodities has its own unique aspect of risk and reward...mother nature.

Cryptocurrency

Cryptocurrency is digital money designed to be used for direct person-to-person transactions over the internet. It is a revolution which began in 2008 with Bitcoin and there are currently over 13,000 different cryptocurrencies available globally.

Cryptocurrency is created through algorithms, and those algorithms rely on cryptography—hence the name cryptocurrency. MAW capital is converted to digital units called "coins." Cryptocurrency makes it possible to transfer the MAW dollar capital globally, 24/7, online without having to use a bank or other institution.

Cryptocurrency is not yet controlled by any government or institutional authority. It is managed by peer-to-peer networks of computers which run the algorithms which are use to convert regular money to digital coins.

The value of cryptocurrency fluctuates based on supply and demand, competition, liquidity, and market sentiment. Because of the lack of government support and regulation and questions about internet security, you need to spend adequate time thoroughly investigating cryptocurrency before you invest.

Collectibles

Collectibles are collections of things that have financial value because they are rare or unusual. What makes a collectible item rare or unusual may be a matter of history, art or special interest. Some common examples are art, rare coins, antiques, automobiles, sports memorabilia and books. Collectibles are a growth investment.

Investing in collectibles can be especially risky because the market for buying and selling collectibles is limited to people who have an interest in a particular item. It is also especially risky because people may invest in collectibles for financial reasons, sentimental reasons or both. So, the market for collectibles can be influenced by human nature as well as by supply and demand. Though there are only six basic categories of investments in your INVEST pocket, remember that there are an infinite number of variations within the six categories to choose from.

Regardless of which investment types you, the sound money habit of regularly investing MAW dollars in your INVEST pocket will enable you to generate the money you will need for long-term goals.

Read quickly now—there are only two last pockets to learn about before your Money Ride adventure begins.

Think About It...

1. What are the sources of investment risk must you consider when investing?
2. How would you diversify a stock portfolio?
3. Which investment category best fits your current long-term financial goals?

8. The Protect Pocket

Expect the Unexpected

There are plenty of potential bumps, bruises and accidents lurking around every corner on the Money Ride—if you're not prepared, they can cost you.

That's why the PROTECT pocket can be the most important pocket on your vest. It's the pocket that "has your back"...that "has you covered." It's the pocket that assures that everything you are trying to achieve financially on the Money Ride won't be derailed by some unexpected loss.

Protection against the risk of unexpected loss is called "insurance," but it really should be called "assurance" because that's what it really provides—the assurance that the wealth-building flow of MAW dollars throughout the pockets on your Opportunity Vest will continue, no matter what unexpected things might happen in your life.

The idea of assurance is important because a loss suffered can generate a negative financial ripple effect throughout the other four vest pockets. Any loss may cause either a direct outflow of SPEND pocket dollars or the ripple effect of having to use SAVE pocket, INVEST pocket—or worse yet—BORROW pocket dollars to cover the loss.

This ripple effect can be as minor as a small additional expense in the SPEND pocket or as serious as entirely stopping the flow of PAW dollars to your vest. Regardless of the degree of loss, an unprotected loss essentially steals MAW dollars from the vest pockets and disrupts the wealth building process.

Regardless of what type of insurance is involved, in the PROTECT pocket, your decisions will be guided by three basic principles: risk transfer, cost sharing and full replacement value.

Health, Income, Property & Life

The four financial domains of potential loss are your health, income, property and life.

Loss of Health

If you have to see a doctor, visit a clinic or go to a hospital because you are sick or injured, you will be charged for any treatment and medicine you receive.

Health insurance is designed to protect you from exposure to medical costs. You will be able to purchase health insurance either under an individual health policy or a group health policy.

You purchase individual coverage personally and pay the entire cost yourself. You can cover yourself as well as your immediate family members under an individual policy.

Group coverage may be available to you if you're a member of a group such as employees of a company or a professional association. Group health coverage is purchased through the group, with the company or professional association paying part of the premium and the employee/association member paying part, and you typically will also pay a portion of the total cost of medial care you receive.

Loss of Income

Except for simply losing your job, income loss is usually caused by an illness or injury. If you are too sick or injured to work, your flow of PAW dollars stops.

Disability income insurance is a form of health insurance that is designed to replace a portion of your income if you are unable to work due to an injury or illness.

This coverage pays a monthly benefit equal to a percentage of your total monthly income, up to a maximum of approximately 66%. The benefit is paid for a stipulated period of time, which varies depending on the type of policy.

Like standard health insurance, you can buy disability insurance using either an individual disability policy or a group disability policy, purchased through an employer or professional association.

Loss of Property

If any of your personal property, real estate, cars or other assets are damaged or lost, there will be a cost to fix or replace the affected property.

Property and casualty insurance is the type of protection you will need as you accumulate assets on the Money Ride. This type of protection pays the cost to replace or repair property such as cars, homes, furnishings and other valuable assets.

This type of insurance may also offer a special type of protection called "personal liability insurance." It is usually offered as part of the coverage on auto and real property insurance policies. Personal liability coverage protects you in the event you accidentally cause a loss or damage to someone's property. It is especially important protection to have as part of your auto insurance—there are some crazy drivers on the Money Ride.

Loss of Life

When you die, anyone who relies on you financially will lose the income you shared with them or used to support them.

This generally includes family members, but can also include business partners who rely on your contributions to the profitability of the company. It's also advisable to have sufficient life insurance protection to pay off any debts you owe.

All insurance is offered by sales agents called representatives or brokers. Sales representatives usually only sell the insurance products offered by a particular company while brokers can sell products offered by many different companies. It is always a good idea to compare companies, products and sales representatives when you shop for insurance.

Risk Transfer

It is a good idea to transfer risk away from yourself whenever possible. This is what insurance does—you pay the insurance company to assume risk.

Insurance protects your PAW and MAW dollars from the cost

of a loss as you rumble along on your Money Ride adventure. For the protection, you will pay the insurance company a fee called a "premium."

Insurance premiums are a fixed expense in your SPEND pocket budget. You can pay insurance premiums annually, semi-annually, quarterly or monthly.

Even if you decide not to buy insurance to transfer a risk, you are still insured, but now you are the insurance company and assume all the risk of loss yourself. It's called being "self-insured." When you are self-insured, you are essentially betting that a certain event is not going to happen.

If you want to be self-insured for any potential loss, you better have a lot of PAW and MAW dollars stashed in your Opportunity Vest. However, if the potential financial loss tied to the event is too great, you may want to reconsider self-insurance and transfer the risk away from yourself...using an insurance company.

Cost Sharing

It is important to know that even if you purchase protection against a potential loss, you won't always be able to transfer 100% of the risk. Depending on the type of coverage you buy, you may have to pay some portion of the cost for health care, repair or replacement the affected asset. On the Money Ride, this is called "cost sharing."

The cost sharing portion you pay under the terms of an insurance policy are typically referred to as the "deductible" and may also include "co-pay" or "out-of-pocket" expenses. The deductible is the portion of the loss/cost you must pay first. The responsibility to pay the balance of the loss/cost is then divided between you and the insurer. Your payment portion is called a "co-payment" and the insurer's portion is called a "claim benefit."

The total amount you have to pay as a deductible payment plus co-payment is limited by the insurance contract to some maximum amount called your total "out-of-pocket" cost. The claim portion you pay is essentially self-insurance where you are the insurance company.

TMR Passenger Tips & Tools #21

Deductibles & Reserves

Deductibles are an important tool in controlling the cost of insurance. It is, however, important that you always have sufficient MAW dollars in your SAVE pocket to cover your deductible exposure. So, when you figure your fixed MAW contribution expense in your monthly budget, be sure to factor in the amount of your deductibles.

Depending upon the type of insurance, you usually have a choice as to the amount of the deductible. The higher the deductible, the more you will pay if a loss occurs. A higher deductible also means that it will cost you less to purchase the insurance because you assume more of the risk.

In the PROTECT pocket, the total potential cost for any insurance is the premiums you pay plus the deductible and co-payment you must pay in the event of a loss. Cost sharing is a useful tool for balancing protection needs with protection costs.

Full Replacement Value

The amount of protection purchased to cover any potential loss should be equal to the cost to entirely restore or replace an affected asset. On the Money Ride, this is called "full replacement value" (FRV).

In some cases, FRV may be the money needed to pay expenses resulting from a loss. In other cases it may be the amount of money needed to replace lost income or repair/replace lost property.

FRV is important because if the amount of protection is not sufficient to cover the cost of the loss, then you may have to use MAW dollars or, worse, borrow money to make up the difference. In this way, FRV protects all of your assets, not just the asset directly affected by a loss.

It is important to use FRV to determine the appropriate amount of protection, because it assures that the wealth-building process throughout your Opportunity Vest can continue if an unexpected loss occurs.

Remember that the risk of unexpected loss is lurking in the shadows at every twist and turn along the Money Ride. But do not fear, because armed with the tools of risk transfer, cost sharing and full replacement value, you'll be able to design your own custom-fitted insurance suit of armor to protect you.

Time is growing short—your ride is about to begin. One last pocket left to explore, but it is just as important as the others, so read carefully.

On to the BORROW pocket!

Think About It...

1. How does "Risk Transfer" work?
2. Which kind of insurance should your currently have?
3. How does "Cost Sharing" work?

9. The Borrow Pocket

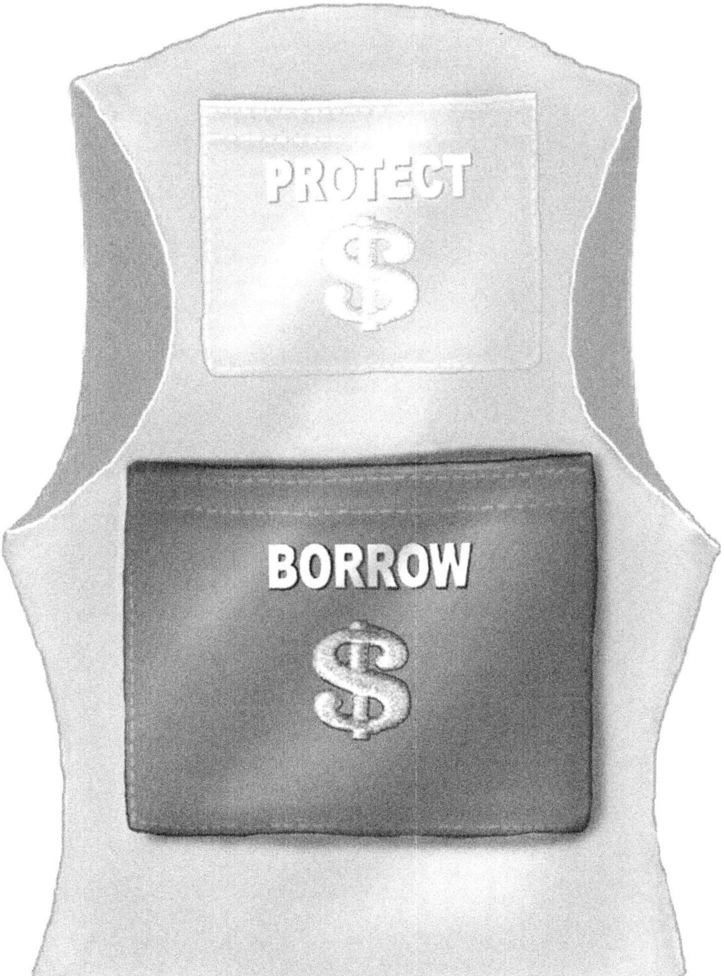

The BORROW pocket is the largest pocket on your Opportunity Vest because your borrowing behavior has the potential to have a positive or negative impact on your financial well-being. Awareness of this good and bad potential of your borrowing decisions is based on the difference between "good debt" and "bad debt." Before we take a closer look at the difference between good and bad debt let's first establish a general understanding of the relationship between credit, debt and loans.

Credit

Credit is a financial resource that enables you to borrow other peoples' money (OPM) to obtain goods and services now for which you pay for later—just like using OPM to purchase real estate in the INVEST pocket. How much OPM you have available to you, i.e., how much a lender will loan you, depends primarily on your credit score and your annual gross income.

Your credit score is basically a lender's view of your trustworthiness—the likelihood that you will repay a debt on time. Credit reports are created by credit reporting agencies using the borrower data they receive from banks, credit card companies and other lenders. The three most often used credit agencies are Equifax, Experian and TransUnion. These consumer reporting companies build your credit report based on your borrowing history. Every time you use your credit to buy something, all transactions associated with that debt are reported to the credit agencies and added to your credit report. The information in your credit report is in turn used to calculate your credit score.

So, how do you establish credit so that you have a viable score to show lenders when you apply for a loan? Go to a bank and open a personal checking account and a savings account. Next, request a credit card from the bank and ask for a card with a credit limit of less than $1,000. Use the card to purchase an inexpensive item such as a pair of jeans. When the credit card bill arrives each month, pay a portion of the balance due, carrying the remaining balance due forward for six months, then pay off the remaining balance. Be sure all payments are made on time to avoid a negative event on your credit history. After the initial six months of carrying the debt, you should pay off credit card debt every month to avoid paying interest on any remaining balance. This approach will create a six-month history of positive borrowing behavior that will be used to calculate your credit score.

The FICO score is a popular scoring system produced by the Fair Isaac Company that uses various aspects of your borrowing behavior to calculate your credit score. FICO scores are based on your borrowing history, generally including how much debt you have, whether you make payments on time, whether you've ever failed to repay a debt, or if you have recently cancelled or added any new debt such as a credit card. FICO scores range from 300 to 850. Every debt transaction has an impact on your credit rating, some big and some small. For example, a single late credit card payment can cause your FICO score to drop by 100 points, and it can take more than a year of good payment history to recover the lost points. If you default on a loan, the default stays on your credit record for up to seven years.

A higher FICO score gives you three advantages: it's easier to qualify for a loan; you'll have lower loan costs for interest and fees; and loan terms can be more flexible. These and other advantages of a higher credit score make it important to check your credit report and score at least every twelve months. You are entitled to one free report per year from each of the three major credit agencies listed above. So, why not use each of the free reports, one every four months? A high credit score is critical to making the most of your turn on the Money Ride by using your credit to create Good Debt when using debt makes sense.

Debt

Debt is the legal obligation of a borrower to repay a lender, at some future time, the principal amount borrowed plus charges for interest and fees. When you use your credit to buy something, you create debt because you are using OPM to make the purchase with the understanding that you must repay the principal amount you borrow plus the amount the lender charges you for the temporary use of OPM.

A debt can be structured many different ways within the general definition, but there are only three basic types of debt: "Revolving debt," where there is no specified repayment date and the unpaid balance revolves to the next payment period, which is typically 30 days. Credit cards are an example of revolving debt. "Installment debt" where there is a specified repayment date and periodic payments consist of part principal repayment and part interest charge. Car loans and student loans are examples of installment debt. "Mortgage debt" which is actually installment debt structured specifically for purchasing real estate like land, houses and buildings. These three debt structures shape the pieces in your total debt puzzle, with each piece representing a separate credit transaction called a "loan."

Loans

Each individual credit transaction which creates a debt is called a "loan." A loan is an agreement that describes the amount borrowed, called the "principal" and the specific loan "terms." The loan terms typically include: the date by which the loan must be fully repaid; the charge to borrow the money, including "interest" and administrative fees; the amount and frequency of payments; any specific responsibilities of the lender and borrower; and penalties for nonperformance for both the lender and the borrower.

Another specific loan term relates to whether a loan is "secured" or "unsecured." A secured loan requires that money or some form of property, called "collateral," be pledged by the borrower so that if the borrower fails to repay a loan and becomes "in default," the lender can legally take ownership of the property pledged as collateral. It is common for the item being purchased with credit to serve as the collateral to secure the loan. Car loans and mortgages are two examples of secured loans.

Unsecured loans require no collateral and use only income and credit history to qualify for the loan. Examples of unsecured loans are bank-issued personal loans, student loans and most credit card purchases.

An important consideration in selecting the type of loan to use is the cost of borrowing. Loan costs are composed of an interest charge plus fees for processing, ongoing service and penalties. The loan's annual interest rate is calculated as a percentage of the loan principal and is charged each payment period. Loan payments are typically monthly. Each loan payment thus consists of part principal repayment and part interest cost.

It is important to know the loan terms and loan costs in order to determine whether a loan is good debt or bad debt and to select the right type of loan and terms for a specific purpose. It's important to note that with every loan the terms are more important than the amount. The amount is easy to determine based on what the money will be used for. It is the terms that describe how the loan obligation will impact your monthly cash flow, total debt load and other financial goals and objectives you are pursuing.

TMR Passenger Tips & Tools #22

Whom Do You Work For?

Having too much debt is like having a second job that doesn't pay you…you pay it.

Some people simultaneously have multiple jobs that cost them instead of paying them. In addition to their regular job, they work for a bank, an auto finance company and one or more credit card companies.

Whom do you work for?

Good Debt

There are three basic criteria for identifying good debt: economic advantage, affordable payments and capacity to repay.

Economic Advantage

Will the loan ultimately generate financial value and/or income? Take a student loan, for example. The promise that "more education equals more income" is the economic advantage of a student loan. The income it produces should far exceed the cost of obtaining the education. But what about a car loan? If a car depreciates in value every year, what's the economic advantage? Maybe, if owning a car was absolutely necessary to earning a living such that you can connect the car and the income; but otherwise, maybe not? Is your credit too valuable a resource to waste on bad debt? Look for the economic advantage and see for yourself.

Affordable Payments

Total monthly debt payments should not exceed a benchmark of 30% of total monthly take-home pay. This will be difficult at times, but benchmarks help keep us responsive to needed adjustments to our financial behavior for the sake of our financial well-being. For many, the rising cost of debt makes affordability tough to keep up with, especially when it comes to credit cards. Excessive or multiple credit card usage automatically qualifies as bad debt.

Capacity to Repay

This is a simple matter of time and money. Do you earn enough income and will you be earning an income long enough to repay the debt? If you don't have a sufficient long-term income stream for repayment, you may need to have enough wealth/collateral that can be sold to generate enough cash to repay the debt. Ideally, you may eventually have the capacity to pay off a debt sooner than required, which will save money on loan interest and fees. This means more money staying in your vest pockets instead of it ending up in the lender's vest pockets.

Bad Debt

If a proposed loan does not meet all three of the good debt criteria, it automatically qualifies as bad debt and should be avoided. The cash flow impact of bad debt can ultimately result in less money in the SPEND, SAVE and INVEST pockets of your Opportunity Vest, compared to what the debt might generate in either income or wealth. Remember the education loan vs. car loan comparison: will the income and/or wealth generated by the debt exceed the cost of the loan repayment plus the lender interest and fees?

Because bad debt leaves you with less money in your vest pockets, it proportionately limits your financial potential, resilience, flexibility and mobility needed to respond to financial opportunity and need — bad debt weighs you down. That's why, on the Money Ride, every bad debt dollar is wrapped around a fireplace brick. Imagine you have a bunch of bricks in your BORROW pocket because you have a car loan you can't afford. Think about how much the weight of the bricks would affect your ability to jump, reach and twist to grab dollars.

Credit cards are what most Money Ride passengers use to get themselves in a jam with bad debt. It usually happens with two critical missteps. First, they use a credit card to spend cash they don't have. Second, they fail to pay off the outstanding balance each month. This means that they have to pay monthly interest on the

> **TMR Passenger Tips & Tools #23**
>
> **Hello...Anyone Home?**
>
> Having to pay credit card interest on something you want but don't need means paying more for the item than if you simply used cash. This is a really good example of bad debt and $-S^2$, Senseless Spending. It is also a good example of what is known on the Money Ride as "self-inflicted inflation."

amount owed until it is paid off. This can in turn lead to the worst situation of all, in which the borrower cannot make the required payments and defaults on the loan.

Sometimes bad debt is the result of originally good debt getting off track due to late payments or "debt creep," where debt increases steadily by small amounts over a long period of time. Other times it may be a single new piece of debt that knocks your total debt situation off balance because now you have too much debt and unaffordable payments. Because it can happen, it's good to have a plan to avoid it before it happens or solve it when it does.

Avoiding bad debt is a matter of using the good debt criteria for evaluating a proposed loan's impact on your general financial well-being. Next, based on the loan terms, select the best loan type for a particular purpose. Finally, based on loan costs, select the lender offering the best terms and most competitive interest rate and fees. Having a process or routine for yourself gives you the best chance to stay on the good side of debt by doing your homework on loan terms before you sign a loan agreement.

If, however, a good debt somehow turns bad, you will need a "fix-it routine" for managing your credit to get it back on track on the good side of debt. Everyone goes through ups and downs on the Money Ride, but being on the bad side of debt is like being hopelessly stuck upside down instead of making progress toward your Money Ride financial goals and objectives.

Since credit cards are a common source of bad debt problems for many people, let's look at some "fix-it routine" tips for dealing with excess credit card debt that has no economic advantage, unaffordable payments or is beyond your repayment capacity.

First, don't panic! It probably took time to get into debt trouble, and it will take time to fix it. As long as there is time, any problem that is fixable is only temporary compared to your long-term financial goals and objectives. It takes a long-term perspective to effectively manage personal finances, and you need to have a routine to follow for solving problems that will give you a sense of progress as you work out solutions.

Contact the lender, explain your financial situation and let them know you are committed to repaying the debt and want to avoid any negative incidents on your credit report. Ask for any help the lender can give, such as temporarily reducing your interest rate or even suspending payments long enough for you to catch up on past due payments. As a last resort, the lender may agree to "settle" your debt by accepting less than you owe to cancel the debt. Beware of this approach, though, because if a lender forgives debt, the amount becomes taxable income to you and the negative event stays on your credit report for seven years.

If the lender can't help you, the next step is to review all of your debt and rank each loan high to low based on the interest charge and fees. Next review all of the variable needs and wants in your monthly budget, identify what you can live without, and calculate how much you can reduce all of your variable spending. This reduced expense amount will be used to accelerate or increase your monthly debt payments.

If you have more than one credit card with a balance due, take the total amount of monthly expenses you are able to cut and use it to increase debt payments starting first with the card with the highest interest charge. You can augment this strategy by simultaneously reducing the monthly payment you pay on other cards to the minimum payment required by the lender until the card with the highest interest charge is paid off. Once the first card is paid off, continue the same monthly payment, shifting it to the next card in line. Be aware that making minimum payments can be very expensive over the long run because interest on the unpaid balance will continue to pile up, and in this example minimum payments are only a temporary measure. Alternatively, if you need more immediate emotional relief from debt stress, you can work on paying off the card with the smallest balance first. Seeing a piece of debt paid off as soon as possible will give your sense of progress a boost.

If a lender can't help and your budget can't produce any excess cash by cutting expenses, it may be possible to transfer the balance to a new credit card with a lower interest charge. Similarly, a personal loan from a bank or a family loan at an interest rate lower than that of the credit card could be used to repay/refinance the credit card balance. (If you use a family loan, make sure the loan is documented properly, as any legal obligation should be.)

A credit repair company can help you evaluate and reorganize your debt, and help make repayment arrangements with lenders. Do your homework to be sure you deal with a reputable company—ask for references.

No matter how effective your bad debt fix-it routine may be, it can't compare to avoiding bad debt all together. That is the purpose of the good debt criteria. The criteria framework provides a consistent approach to dealing with sometimes difficult choices, and the objective is to always use good debt.

Make the most of your turn on the Money Ride by using and not abusing your BORROW pocket. Optimize your credit resource by using good debt for lifestyle and wealth-building in concert with all of the other pockets on your Opportunity Vest.

Think About It...

1. What are the three criteria of 'Good Debt"?

2. How does "Bad Debt" limit your financial success?

3. What are two methods for paying off excess credit card debt?

10. Time to Buckle Up!

Before you buckle up, now that you've covered all of the basics in the five domains of money behavior on your Opportunity Vest, let's look at an approach to making smart money decisions you can use to keep your decisions aligned with your financial goals.

First, know your money self and know that as human beings, we all have a limited intellectual ability—you can't think of everything you need to know to make good decisions. Know what you want from a decision in terms of money and your personal preferences which reflect your moral values and experiences related to money.

Next, know that all financial decisions deal with spending time and money to satisfy needs and wants, time, money and your preferences. Time can be expressed in terms of decision deadlines or the time it takes to execute a decision immediately, in the moment or over a period of years.

Money can be a decision's cost or reward. Cost can happen at the front end of a decision or as an ongoing expense paid over months or years or at a future date. Reward can also be in the form of some specific non-money preference related to your morals or emotions such as feeling financially secure, safe from risk.

Regardless of whether your expected reward is expressed in dollars or as an expression of some moral value, you need to be clear on what you need and want. You also need to be committed to making a decision and taking the actions needed to execute it such as with routines for budgeting or investing.

In summary with everything you have learned about the five domains of money behavior, here are five steps to making smart money decisions that you can use to guide your decision-making routine:

1. Have a clear idea of what you want to accomplish financially and make a real commitment to make a decision and to follow through with execution to completion.

2. Identify the reward you expect to receive from the decision in terms of how it will make you feel about your financial well-being. Remember that experiences are important to our happiness and that spending money only on material goods can deprive you of valuable life experiences.

3. Be aware of risk and probability decisions. Everyone is naturally risk averse, but remember time can offset risk, especially in investing. A longer a time horizon can turn a relatively risky short-term investment into a long-term gain.

4. Compare solution options looking for the most efficient use of money applied to the decision. Be willing to compromise on your preferences in case no single option is perfect, but be sure the compromise does not sacrifice efficiency.

   Before a final decision, ask yourself whether there is something more important that you could use the subject money for. Looking at a decision from a different point of view can help clarify cost, reward and preference.

5. Design a routine that you can use to guide your money behavior toward completion of your decisions. Monitor your routine and evaluate the decision based on the future rewards you expect the decision to produce rather than by the initial or past costs paid.

OK, you're all set, ready to start your turn. You have the know-how and know-what you need to make the most of your turn…time to start grabbing!

Welcome to the Money Ride, it's the ride of a lifetime and we're all on it!

Glossary of Money Ride Terms

Bad Debt Any debt that is unaffordable in terms of the payments and/or the repayment.

Borrowing Score Also known as FICO score. Scoring system used to determine a person's credit worthiness based upon their borrowing activity.

Cash Flow Money flowing into the Opportunity Vest as income and out as expenses.

Chasm of Financial Despair The chasm separating PAW and MAW representing the unhappiness caused by the failure to spend less than one earns.

Compounding The accumulation of money created by the continual crediting of interest on principal and on the interest earned in the prior periods.

Financing Borrowing money either to purchase goods and services or to acquire assets.

Fixed Expenses Expenses which reoccur for the same amount each month.

Good Debt Debt which is affordable and which creates a financial advantage.

MAW Money at Work. Excess earnings invested to generate growth and/or income as part of the wealth-building process.

Money Dynamics The roles and rules of money which govern the efficient use of money.

Money I.Q. Knowledge and understanding of how money works and the ability to successfully apply that knowledge to a lifetime of money choices and decisions.

Money Person Personality type described in terms of behavior regarding money.

Money Routine A sequence of actions designed to complete a task for a specific purpose.

Money Supply Amount of spendable cash available in the SPEND and SAVE pockets.

OPM Other Peoples' Money; money borrowed using credit cards or loans.

PAW People at Work, generating income by direct labor, a job, work etc.

Ripple Effect The positive or negative effect of one dollar transaction on the other dollars in the money supply.

Risk Tolerance A person's capacity to emotionally and financially assume the risk of loss.

Sound Money Habit A pattern of money behavior designed to accomplish a specific purpose or goal.

Smart Money Decisions Financial decisions using thoughtful consideration of money and time, to satisfy needs, wants and goals.

Staging Coordinating the liquidity timeline of various savings vehicles with the timeline of the proposed uses for the money.

Today Dollars PAW and MAW dollars which are needed for current expenses.

Tomorrow Dollars MAW dollars in the SAVE and INVEST pockets designated for future uses.

Variable Expenses Monthly expenses for needs or wants which vary from month to month based on consumption.

Vest Dynamics The mechanics of money affecting the flow of dollars throughout the pockets on the Opportunity Vest.

Wealth Wealth is property also called "assets," which have a money value, can grow in value or can generate income.

Work I.Q. All of the education, job skills and personal skills you acquire that enable you to earn an income.

About the Author

William K. Busch is a personal finance educator and public speaker.

Bill has spent the past 30 years as a financial advisor helping clients make smart money decisions to address a variety of financial issues and concerns.

He has utilized the diversity of his professional expertise and his background as a business educator to present educational outreach workshops on personal finance for community groups, companies and schools.

This book is the culmination of his professional experiences working with clients and his years of developing techniques for teaching the fundamentals of money and wealth.

For more information on *The Money Ride*,
and to order additional copies of this book,
please visit

www.TheMoneyRide.com

Made in the USA
Monee, IL
04 November 2026

67379777R00075